Praise for Career of Gold

The golden generation needs Career of Gold *in a big way! Bracken combines wonderful inspiration and practical direction for anyone in his or her 50's, 60's, 70's and even older who wants another career but doesn't know where to begin.*
—JULIE JENSEN, AUTHOR OF *I DON'T KNOW WHAT I WANT, BUT I KNOW IT'S NOT THIS.*

Career of Gold *redefines the term "golden years." It is a very interesting and timely book.*
—JOHN DOWNES, AUTHOR, *BARRON'S DICTIONARY OF FINANCIAL TERMS.*

"Career of Gold *is a book that inspires those in their golden years who need to build a financial security and then shows them how to go about it using new technology as their means. A very timely book that recognizes a growing need in our country. If you are wondering 'Am I too old for this?'* Career of Gold *will give you the reassurance and support you need to move forward."*
—AZRIELA JAFFE, AUTHOR OF 14 BOOKS, INCLUDING *HONEY I WANT TO START MY OWN BUSINESS*

Career of Gold *wins a gold medal for timing.*
There has never been a better time for a
book like this to appear. It's a winner.
—PEGGY MCCOLL, AUTHOR OF *THE 8 PROVEN SECRETS TO*
SMART SUCCESS.

Career of Gold *is a fourteen carat book of insight for*
the person over fifty who is seeking a new career.
It is a book that encourages, inspires and directs.
It is a book, too, for people ready for success.
—RANDY GILBERT, FOUNDER OF *INSIDESUCCESSRADIO.COM*

The bravery of living requires everyone to learn from
seeing the examples of other people's behavior. Don
Bracken teaches us how to be willing to take a chance
while minimizing the risk of facing the unknown.
Bracken provides, in his own creative way, the
optimistic vote for the future which is essential for
both the individual and for society itself.
—GIDEON G. PANTER, M.D.
CLINICAL ASSOCIATE PROFESSOR, OBS/GYN, WEILL-CORNELL
MEDICAL COLLEGE OF CORNELL UNIVERSITY
AUTHOR: *NOW THAT YOU'VE HAD YOUR BABY,*
CO-AUTHOR: *PREGNANCY AND CHILDBIRTH,*
FORMER MONTHLY COLUMNIST *PARENTS MAGAZINE.*

CAREER OF GOLD

Disclaimer

This book is designed to provide information on establishing a career in one's golden years. It is sold with the understanding that the publisher and author are not engaged in rendering legal, accounting or other professional services. If legal or other expert assistance is required, the services of a competent professional should be sought.

It is not the purpose of this book to provide all the information that is otherwise available to those launching a new career, but instead to complement, amplify and supplement other texts. You are urged to read all the available material, learn as much as possible about all the recommended aspects and tailor the information to your individual needs. For more information, see the many resources in the back of the book.

Every effort has been made to make this book as complete and as accurate as possible. However, there *may be mistakes,* both typographical and in content. Therefore, this text should be used only as a general guide and not as the ultimate source of launching a new career. Furthermore, this book contains information that is current only up to the printing date.

The purpose of this book is to is to educate, entertain and encourage. The author and Today's Books shall have neither liability nor responsibility to any person or entity with respect to any loss or damage caused, or alleged to have been caused, directly or indirectly, by the information contained in this book.

If you do not wish to be bound by the above, you may return this book to the publisher for a full refund.

Don Bracken

CAREER OF GOLD

Defeat Age Bias By Re-Careering
For The Second Half Of Your Life.

Using the knowledge you have gained in your life
to build a new career in your post-fifty years. One that will give
you fulfillment, security and the recognition you deserve.

Today's Books
an imprint of
History Publishing Company, LLC
Palisades, NY

Career of Gold
Starting Your New Career
Defeat Age Bias By Re-Careering For The Second Half Of Your Life.
by Don Bracken

Cover and interior design by 1106 Design
Editing by 1106 Design

Published by Today's Books, an imprint of
History Publishing Company, LLC
PO Box 700, Palisades, NY 10964-0700
(845) 359-1765
SAN 850–5942

ISBN 978-1-933909-84-6 Print ed.
ISBN 978-1-933909-85-4 PDF ed.

Library of Congress Cataloging-in-Publication Data

Bracken, Don
Career of Gold

Library of Congress Control Number: 2006926783

Includes bibliographical references(p.) and index.

To June, Chuck and Don

who are always digging for the gold

It is a mistake to regard age as a downhill grade toward dissolution. The reverse is true. As one grows older, one climbs with surprising strides.
—GEORGE SAND

I have enjoyed greatly the second blooming... suddenly you find—at the age of 50, say—that a whole new life has opened before you.
— AGATHA CHRISTIE

Aging is not 'lost youth' but a new stage of opportunity and strength.
—BETTY FRIEDAN

ACKNOWLEDGEMENTS

This is an uncomplicated book. It was written with that intention because the times in which we live are complicated. In order to deal with those issues and complications, it helps greatly to have a clear understanding of how to go about it. It was said by the prominent English editor George Buckle, that simplicity is the first essential of success. Hopefully it will prove true here.

It takes a lot of people to make such a book: editors, designers, contributors, printers… well the list could go on so I will start my list right now. Firstly I wish to thank Ross Perot and George Foreman, two people I have long admired for their ability to rise above the rest of us with not just rare and disciplined talent but to do so with dignity and a smile. They are both great role models for independent enterprise.

So too, five wonderful people who have brought their stories to this work. Cynthia Riggs who has brought many a smile and the excitement of mystery to her readers as she whisks them to Martha's Vineyard with her wonderful novels; Jacqueline Marcell, author and activist who has worked endlessly for the elderly and brought attention to an area that has long demanded it; Dennis Myers and Lynne Colwell who have found their destinies in reinventing themselves and are examples to all of us; and Jude Wright who has found her destiny by helping others in so many different ways.

Thanks very much to Jack Canfield, Dr. Joyce Brothers and Harvey Mackay for their contributions and wisdom. My thanks also to prolific authors Azriella Jaffe and Julie Jensen for their support and kind words of encouragement; author Peggy McColl and radio host Randy Gilbert for their invaluable help in bringing this book and so many others to public attention and to best-selling author and financial expert John Downes who early on pointed out the rising financial difficulties the post-fifty generation will be experiencing. And a special thanks too, to distinguished physician and author Gideon Panter whose specialty focuses on the beginning of life but whose sagacious observations about the totality of life brought perspective to my efforts.

Thanks also to David Seeger, video expert and good neighbor for his technical input; Antoinette Kuritz, publicist and friend who offered invaluable insight and direction, Sheila Asch for her constructive commentary as this book progressed and Amy Collins who brought a light to the dark byways of book distribution.

And very importantly, my thanks to those people who brought technical and production expertise to the book: Michele DeFilippo for her patience and artful design inside and out; Steve Sirlin for his patient guidance on book production; and Kate von Seeburg for her editing skill and tireless eye.

Lastly to everyone who kept reassuring me that this is a book that should be written: my sons Chuck and Don, daughter-in-law Liz, great friend June Starke, and all my over-fifty friends and neighbors who conviced me that the time was right for *Career of Gold*.

Table of Contents

To the Reader

What is a career of gold? It is taking the knowledge and work skills that you have learned in your first 50, 60, 70 years or more and coupling them with the subject that interests you above all others creating a synergetic force of information that can be marketed through today's easy-to-use technology.

This is the time of life like no other. You have more wisdom, skills and self-knowledge than at any other time of your life. Now is the time to "put it all together."

I have put this book together because I have done just that and it is not a difficult thing to do. I did it twice.

At age 55, I set up, owned and ran a distribution company for a large Texas conglomerate serving the New York Metropolitan area and in the process earned several million dollars.

At age 65, after leaving my business, I started another: the History Publishing Company, a firm focusing on developing classroom aids to give students an immediate comprehension of complex subjects using the American Civil War as the initial project.

An award winning book, *Times of the Civil War,* followed and a series of books are being prepared to follow the classroom aids. That was one of my interests.

Another interest emerged lately when some friends of mine experienced bias in the workplace. It was then that I came to realize the huge bias that exists in our culture against those of us who are over fifty.

This book is the result of that realization.

Career of Gold is for those of us who are concerned about our future but are uncertain how to deal with it, particularly in this time of fast moving technological change.

Career of Gold is a guide that will give you insight and direction in this modern day marketplace. If you wish to do something more with your life, the timing for a career has never been better. You are a valuable person who has much to give and your sense of judgement is probably better than ever.

That said, go for it. Go for the gold.

When you stop giving and offering something to the rest of the world, it's time to turn out the lights.
—GEORGE BURNS

CHAPTER 1

WHAT A CAREER OF GOLD WILL DO FOR YOU

Cynthia Riggs of Martha's Vineyard, Massachusetts, had her first novel published when she was 70 years old. Five years later she had finished seven more and is now busily working on another.

Dennis Myers of Laguna Beach, California, a corporate executive at age 54, reinvented his life when he was widowed. Ten years later at age 64 he had become a chef, writer and coach and is living in his dream house.

Michelle Beaudry at age 52 was a comedienne. She made the move into hypnosis and now practices hypnotherapy, helping others to get their personal power back to overcome anger, lose weight and stop smoking.

Cynthia, Dennis and Michelle are but a few of the thousands who have re-careered in their post-fifty years. They were concerned about their future and took action. You will meet them later. Their stories and others are in this book.

You may be reading this book because you are concerned about your future because more than a few years are behind you. You may be bored or feeling a lack of fulfillment, or money may be a matter of concern. If any of those reasons apply, you have every right to be concerned but not to the point of despair because you may be entering the most potent years of your life.

If you are north of 50 years, you are in the so-called golden years. TV commercials run by insurance companies picture us on the beach, basking in the golden rays of sun in the twilight of our lives. Other commercial images depict two gray haired folk walking hand in hand down the country lane, the sun's golden rays dappled about them, old folks to be humored and coddled.

Thanks, but no thanks.

This book is for the individuals who know that the nudge those people are getting in those commercials is into the shadows of their lives.

In 1992, Peter Drucker, a leading exponent of business management, wrote in *Psychology Today:*

> "Peter Drucker: Here I am, 58, and I still don't know what I am going to do when I grow up. My children and their spouses think I am kidding when I say that, but I am not. Nobody tells them that life is not that

categorized. And nobody tells them that the only way to find what you want is to create a job. Nobody worth his salt has ever moved into an existing job. There are a few elementary things you can do first."

And finding yourself is probably one of them. If Peter Drucker wasn't sure what he was going to do when he "grew up," don't feel bad. There is hope for the rest of us.

The golden years.

You can call them the golden years—and they are, but not the way the insurance folks would have you believe.

The meaning is changing because times are changing and the gold in the golden years is taking on a new reality. It is, or can become, the real thing. This time of life can be a golden opportunity, that is, it can be if you think it can be, and if you do, your golden opportunity may be just in front of you.

Why? Because you probably have something other people want. And that's the knowledge you have gained over the years. To some, it is very valuable knowledge.

> *If you have knowledge,*
> *let others light their candles with it.*
> —WINSTON CHURCHILL

Deep within your subconscious lies the vast reservoir of knowledge that you have accumulated during your life. Every minute of experience and exposure is recorded there, but I am rushing ahead. I will digress.

We have spent several decades of our lives acquiring skills in various lines of work. Word processing, mountain climbing guide, lawyer and dress designing are a few of the thousands of skills you may have developed in order to sustain yourself and your family. In so doing, you probably contributed to the dreams and ambitions of others and marginally to yourself. Perhaps little thought was given to following your star, or fulfilling your dream. If you did give some thought to it, you probably shelved it with the intention of getting to it sometime down the road.

Or maybe other things like getting married, supporting yourself or your family, meeting the onslaught of life, have been the things that took you on the course you pursued, a course that prompted you to shelve your dreams. It was a course that may have been rationally correct at the time. Obligations had to be met, bread and butter came first not to mention the mortgage, cars, kids' education and the rest.

But if you did dwell on following your star, it may have been a momentary flash of wishful thinking that you put aside in order to meet your obligations. And that you may have done by pushing others forward and upward.

In the process, you climbed a few hills as you pushed others up the mountain but you never tried to climb the mountain for yourself. Did you? Admit it now. Don't go into denial.

But we are rushing ahead. Perhaps you have made a climb for yourself and discovered that your personal mountain was not quite high enough. Having climbed to the top you may have the need to scale new heights. Or perhaps it was an easy climb and you have a need for a new challenge. Other factors may have presented themselves, too: a premature decision to indulge in the lifestyle of "retirement" may have resulted in a lifestyle of boredom instead, and you want to go back to the real world; or perhaps what you are doing now is just plain boring and you want the stimulation and excitement of your own business endeavor.

There are myriad personal reasons for opting for a career of gold, and they all encompass all or some of the qualities of stimulation, excitement and reward.

Accept your own personal challenge and another mountain, a career of gold, will await your climb.

Living by proxy is always a precarious expedient.
—SIMONE DE BEAUVOIR

Now you are at an age and a time when it just may be possible to climb that mountain.

Are you "half-thinking" or thinking about doing it now?

If your answer to the former is yes, keep thinking. If it is the latter, your own personal Matterhorn may be just in front of you.

And it probably will look steeper than it really is.

But you can still climb the thing. So look upward. You can still climb it. It is not too late.

Financed by his $105 Social Security check, Colonel Harland Saunders started his chicken empire when he was 65. And all with just a recipe in hand.

And Anna Mary Robertson, when her hands turned arthritic at 80, turned from needlework to painting and became the nation's foremost practitioner of Naif art, the work of artists in sophisticated societies who reject conventional expertise in the depiction of real objects.

By the time she died at the age of 105 she had produced more than 2000 paintings, all carrying a big price tag. Her work appears in museums and galleries and if you want to see her work, when you go into an art museum, ask for the Grandma Moses section.

If you accept your own personal challenge as Anna Mary Robertson or Harland Saunders did, you will find an exhilaration in climbing for yourself.

As you start off, you will probably be nervous, maybe even a little frightened, but that will be good. Your adrenaline will be flowing, you will be wide awake and action oriented.

There is no magic or illusion on these pages, just reality laced with pragmatism. The suggestions and directions are based on real happenings that helped this writer and other successful people turn corners and climb upward during their golden years.

So, once you start your climb, any uncertainty that you have will leave you because you will have direction and a formula to follow.

The mountain always seems highest before the first step is taken. But before that first step is taken, it is important to know why the journey is necessary. There are reasons that may surprise you. They are just ahead.

Retirement at sixty-five is ridiculous. When I was sixty-five I still had pimples.

—GEORGE BURNS

Thoughts

1. The Federal Reserve Board's report, "National Survey of Small Business Finances (1995)," found that small businesses (fewer than 500 employees) were home-based 53 percent of the time.

2. It also found that 24 percent of all new businesses in 1993 began with no outside financing.

3. Although many people believe that 80 percent of all small businesses fail within five years, statistics from the U. S. Census Bureau reveal a different story. The Census Bureau reports that 76 percent of all small businesses operating in 1992 were still in business in 1996. In fact, only 17 percent of all small businesses that closed in 1997 were reported as bankruptcies or other failures. The other 83 percent of the terminations occurred because the business was sold or incorporated or the owner retired. The odds for success are very good.

4. The power to start your career of gold and to climb your mountain is in your mind. And that power is in your subconscious which is the repository of all your thoughts. How you feel about yourself is in your subconscious. Your energy, financial outlook, social environment, political perspective and positive or negative attitudes are all there.

5. Beliefs can be changed. Negative outlooks can be changed to positives. If you recognize negative influences in your thinking, you must make the change. You can do it. Read ahead.

Though no one can go back and make a
brand new start, anyone can start from now
and make a brand new ending.

—CARL BARD

CHAPTER 2

YOUR GOLDEN OPPORTUNITY
IS AT HAND

Your golden career can be had because of the nature of things today. Twenty years ago it was very difficult, almost impossible to do what can be done today. You might say, the career of gold is possible because of the golden opportunities at hand.

Those opportunities consist of using the skills you have acquired to help others meet their needs. You can now use them to follow your own dream by implementing them with what you were meant to do.

You can use them to launch your career of gold, to find the success and fulfillment you deserve. Because of the abundant changes in technology and our culture, there has never been a better time to do that than now.

If you are bored with early retirement and want to get back in the action, opportunity awaits you.

If you want a better way of life and a better cash flow and if you want something better than packing groceries at the A&P, you can now take action to get that better life.

If you are in retirement and want to realize that sense of fulfillment you may never have experienced but are not quite sure what would give you that fulfillment, read ahead. Some of the techniques for discovering the source of that fulfillment will be examined.

There are also very good reasons why you should pursue a career of gold and those reasons are explored in the chapters ahead. Some may startle you but if you have the right attitude, they can work to your advantage.

And taking advantage of them now is very possible if you have the right attitude.

Now that may read like circular reasoning but attitude is critical; it is the underlying factor in entrepreneurship or self-employment.

Call it what you will. Self-employment, working primarily as an individual or entrepreneur, starting and building a business is what the career of gold is all about.

It is your mountain that is being climbed and you are pulling yourself up, not pushing someone else. When the results are in, it is you who will be standing on the top and the profits and the recognition will be yours. This is a great time to achieve these things.

A great wind is blowing, and that gives you
either imagination or a headache.
—CATHERINE THE GREAT

Thoughts

1. Change is the essence of opportunity and it comes in so many ways that you may sometimes feel you are enveloped in them. If you are looking for a change to light your way to opportunity, look for solid state lighting (LED). It will also be lighting up your life one day in the near future or at least where brightness, visibility and long-life are important, such as in exit signs and traffic signals.

2. LEDs are just one opportunity that is on the verge of making an impact. There are more. There has never been a better time to climb the mountain to success than now. Opportunity is all around you and the channels to those opportunities are wide open.

3. Your attitude will determine your success. The law of cause and effect will dictate the results. Positive begets positive, negative begets negative. That's as old a thought as the Old Testament.

4. You can program your attitude. You can change negative to positive providing you are aware of your negative outlook. You can achieve at any age anything you set out to do…if you believe you can do it, you can do it.

5. Your attitude controls your life in every respect. A positive attitude determines your response to adversity; it pushes you back up when life knocks you down and when you keep getting up, life will look for easier opponents.

Why You Should Pursue a Career of Gold

Reason One – You Are Living Longer and Longer

The tooth grows longer and longer. You will be living longer than expected. The extra years gives you the time to build that golden career.

You are living more years because of better nutrition and healthcare. The intake of better foodstuffs is giving your body a longer lasting vibrancy and your increasing awareness of what is in the foods you eat. If you read those little panels on food packaging, you will probably agree that they are very helpful.

The government watchdogs at the Food and Drug Administration are on the alert for you, too. They are consistently warning you, via the six o'clock news, about the downside of some highly advertised pharmaceuticals like the recent flap over Vioxx.

If joint pain is your problem though, there is remedy for that. Vioxx may be on the bench but there are a host of over-the-counter arthritis pain pills on the sidelines waiting to rush in to give you relief. And doctors are quick to make appropriate recommendations.

And there are the never-ending developments in medical care that's keeping you on the upswing. Every year there appears to be a major breakthrough in healthcare. Your vaccinations, antibiotics, newly developed treatments, testing procedures and surgical remedies are not only prolonging your life, they are keeping you in good shape.

The U. S. Census Bureau says that if you were born in 1935, you were expected to live to the ripe age of 61. Today in the year 2006, your life expectancy is 76 and in another 25 years it will be 80.

And beyond that, how about 100?

The U. S. Census estimates that there are 54,000 people over 100 years of age now and the Bureau is now keeping count of those who have passed the 110 year mark.

You could have the longest career of your life ahead of you.

Tires you just to think of it, doesn't it?

My friend Peter, a grayhaired writer who spent several decades writing for a world class magazine, says that the one thing that he needs more than anything else is energy.

Think then of over-the-counter vitamin supplements like Centrum® Silver® specially designed for the golden generation. Among other things, it converts food consumption to energy.

I use the stuff every day and if I don't use it, I tire around 3 p.m., but with it I have energy the entire day. Let's face it, the body does change and when you reach 50 or so, it slows down in the production of certain nutrients. Knowing what supplements to take and when to take them can enhance your lifestyle and adds an uptick to personal production.

So you've got a long way to go baby. And you can get there too.

So pop those pain pills and your Centrum® Silver® and move ahead. There's a full day ahead of you. Make every moment of it count.

> *Within us all there are wells of thought and dynamos*
> *of energy which are not suspected until emergencies*
> *arise. Then oftentimes we find that it is comparatively*
> *simple to double or triple our former capacities and to*
> *amaze ourselves by the results achieved.*
>
> —THOMAS J. WATSON

Thoughts

1. The Food Safety and Inspection Service (FSIS) advised consumers in early 2006 that cooking raw poultry to a minimum internal temperature of 165°F will eliminate pathogens and viruses. On the surface of things that doesn't seem like much but it is the little things that add up. And that is one reason we are living longer. You are probably going to be living a lot

longer than you thought. More and more people are living past 100 years of age. Even 110.

2. You've got a long way to go. Keep in shape, take your nutrients. Life can be good, even great. As you move through the years you will gain in wisdom and experience. During your golden years, your sense of judgement will be better than at any time of life. That's an established fact.

3. Your gray hair will be a symbol of that wisdom but you will be the age you think you are. You have much to give. As you experience more in life, you will have much more to give to those younger than you and those less experienced.

4. The wisdom you have attained and the knowledge you have stored in your subconscious warehouse is of value to many others. Share it with them. They will gladly pay for it.

Reason Two – Your Need For Money Grows Every Year

You've got to pay for those extra years. Call this the great motivator.

Because of better nutrition and healthcare there is going to be a need for you to finance the longer life you are leading and this should be of major concern. You may be financially secure and if you are, you are a step ahead. But if you are not financially prepared to finance those extra years, you are not alone. Indications are that most Americans are not in good financial shape.

Many baby boomers, soon to be pouring into the golden generation, will be sitting on the wobbly three legged stool of Social Security, pensions and private savings. And the legs are wobbly indeed.

If you are preparing to sit on that stool, watch out. Social Security is under close scrutiny and will be overhauled with less benefits in the near future. That is a certainty. There will be too few people working in the future to carry the overload of people drawing Social Security benefits. Many corporations public and private are reeling under the overload of pension liability and the future does not bode well for pensioners who are constantly seeing cutbacks in pension payouts. The Ford Motor Company's recent cutback in retirees' healthcare benefits, General Motor's buyout offer to its 100,000 employees of Delphi (its former subsidiary) and the City of San Diego's shortchanging its employees' pension system are three strong indicators of trouble ahead.

There are plenty of good five cent cigars in the country.
The trouble is they cost a quarter.
—FRANKLIN P. ADAMS, POET AND NEWSPAPER COLUMNIST

The end result is that many people approaching retirement are putting it off and those already retired or between engagements, as some might say, are having a tough time making ends meet.

If that's you, just how tough is it getting?

Let's take a look and a guess.

Demos, a nonpartisan group that studies economics and election reform, reported in its study "Retiring in the Red" that seniors are increasingly incurring debt just to make ends meet. Taking a close look at the economic security of different populations pertaining to debt, assets and major costs between 1989 and 2001, the report stated that nearly one in three senior credit card holders carry debt due to low incomes that stagnated or declined during the '90s while basic costs increased.

The study taken from the Federal Reserve's Survey of Consumer Finances stated that the average self-reported credit card debt among seniors increased by 89 percent between 1992 and 2001, the hardest hit group, the 65–69, up a staggering 217 percent.

And the increase on those basic costs just referred to? Here's a few food examples culled from the Consumer Price Index going from 1990 to 2005: tomatoes up 201 percent, oranges 141 percent, butter 91 percent, lamb 71 percent, chicken 68 percent.

Has your 1990 income doubled to cover the cost of butter or tripled to cover the cost of tomatoes?

Hopefully it has but if you were retired, enough said.

The question isn't at what age I want to retire,
it's at what income.
—GEORGE FOREMAN

Thoughts

1. Money is in huge supply in the economy. M1, one of the principal measurements of that supply was reported by the Federal Reserve to be $1,375.1 billion in February, 2006. That is an amazing amount of money and with decent planning you can get some of it. It is a matter of attitude.

2. Money is a good thing. It allows you to provide for your needs and your family's wants. Having money can help bring enjoyment to your life and the wise use of it can help lead to a balanced and pleasant life.

3. The wise use of money also brings serenity to your life. It is that serenity that brings peace of mind and helps maintain good physical health. The attainment of money and a sense of fulfillment should be the end result of your career of gold.

4. If you follow the formula for success shown at the back of this book, it will be possible to have a career that will bring you the money, serenity and peace of mind that you deserve.

Reason Three – You Are Smarter Than Ever

*The older I get, the greater power I seem to have
to help the world; I am like a snowball—
the further I am rolled, the more I gain.*

—Susan B. Anthony

Your judgement is better than ever. You are better than ever.

Yes you are and recent studies of emotional intelligence, the application of intelligence and emotion in the workplace, shows it.

You have years of experience tempered by the slings, arrows, travails and other forms of weaponry life has chosen to throw at you. You may be able to handle things in a way you couldn't when you were 20 or 30 years younger. Perhaps you had to deal with overcharges of emotion when you were in your 30s or 40s that you now have under control. Maturity may have brought you wisdom not only of the skills you have developed over the years but how best to use those skills in conjunction with other people. You may be at the top of your form.

Believe it.

If you have been taking care of yourself nutritionally, getting proper exercise and keeping your mind reasonably active, you may be the best you have ever been. Experience has taken you there.

Yes, you have the aches and pains of life, you've got to pop your arthritis pain killers and your Centrum Silver® but you do that without question because you accept reality. And your emotional intelligence probably reflects it.

Yes, unlike IQ which is set and unchangeable from childhood on, Emotional Intelligence (EI), which is the harmonizing of intellect and emotion, usually increases with age and maturity.

The business community was shocked when research showed that 90 percent of one's performance effectiveness was due to emotional savvy rather than technological knowledge. That's EI.

If you are not familiar with the background of it, Emotional Intelligence is a relatively new term coined by Peter Salovey of Yale and John Mayer of the University of New Hampshire in 1990. They defined the term as the capacity for recognizing our own feelings and those of others, for motivating ourselves, and for managing emotions well in ourselves and in our relationships.

In a more succinct fashion Hendrie Weisinger defined it simply as "the intelligent use of our emotions." And when you intentionally make your emotions work for you by using them to help guide your behavior and thinking in ways that enhance your results, you are scoring high on the EI charts.

> *Maturity: Be able to stick with a job until it is finished. Be able to bear an injustice without having to get even. Be able to carry money without spending it. Do your duty without being supervised.*
>
> —ANN LANDERS

It is vitally important to understand yourself and why you may have made the career choices you did make in the past if they were unhappy choices. Equally important, an awareness of your emotional intelligence will better enable you to make the choices you will make in formulating your golden career.

In his groundbreaking book *Emotional Intelligence* which first appeared in 1995 and which you should read, Daniel Goleman points out that when technology was developed allowing brain imaging, it brought an insight into the intricate workings of the brain that allowed psychologists to better understand the processes within you that stimulated your thinking and feeling.

Goleman touches on the things that you of the golden generation have been working on these past years: the ability to better understand your emotions and how your emotions have been at work all your life. They were set in place by your earliest teachers in the classroom and at home. You were wired with your emotional circuitry there and it was continued through your adolescence. Guilt at displeasing a parent was probably a big one and a host of others were set in place as well.

The emotional responses you experienced throughout life had a controlling effect, sometimes resulting in poor career moves.

People don't choose their careers;
they are engulfed by them.
—JOHN DOS PASSOS, AUTHOR

All emotions are impulses to act. They are immediate plans for dealing with life that God and nature has installed in you. Some are negative—the type that drives you away from something, and others are positive—the type that drives you to something. Since every action you take is driven by an emotionally charged decision, you must know how you think before you make your move to your career of gold.

No, this is not getting heavy. You will be surprised at how light the process actually is.

Knowing how you think is possible only if you know why you are thinking what you are thinking. True, it is not always an easy thing to do for some of those emotions that have fostered the decisions in the first place are not always evident. Some are working entangled with others while others try to overwhelm you for no apparent reason. It is a matter of being aware of them.

Since they are the driving forces in every decision you have made in the past and will make in the future, you must take a look at them in Chapter Ten.

> *The greatest discovery of my generation*
> *is that a human being can alter his life*
> *by altering his attitudes of mind.*
> —WILLIAM JAMES

Thoughts

1. Emotions are the driving force of life. Your emotional intelligence is the driver and it springs from your subconscious. Your subconscious accepts what is given it by the conscious mind. Your conscious mind rationalizes and makes decisions. Those decisions are sent to the subconscious as truths as the conscious deems them to be.

2. Emotional Intelligence is developed largely by experience and awareness. If you are over 50, you are probably smart, have experience, and understand life better than you ever have. Your Emotional Intelligence is probably at a high level.

3. Emotional Intelligence gives you control. Acting in a positive, unruffled way in the face of negativity and criticism will give you control of the situation. You have probably developed this skill and are much better at it than the younger people in your life.

Reason Four – There Is Bias Against You – Use It

Yes, it will save you valuable time and I am sure that you are wondering just how bias fits into this. Bias against the golden generation is the single largest form of prejudice in the United States, surpassing race and gender. "It is the largest bias we see," said Dr. Mahazarin Banaji, Social Ethics professor at Harvard University when interviewed by the Harvard University *Gazette*.

Using brain scans and online testing initiated in 1998, Professor Banaji and her colleagues have studied the results of 40,000 tests which showed the prejudice that Americans have for the golden generation.

How did this come to be? Ironically, at several points, you have probably bought into it and helped perpetuate it, too.

You certainly have if you have purchased a birthday card for someone over 50 which mockingly laughed at failing eyesight, wrinkles, thinning or disappearing hair and all the rest.

If you have watched a television show and characters over 50 were depicted as doddering sorts, hard of hearing or highly myopic and you failed to write the producer a note of criticism, you have passively accepted the stereotype. And if you discounted a very elderly person as being "not quite with it," when engaged in a circle of conversation, you have definitely bought into it.

> *Prejudice and self-sufficiency naturally proceed from inexperience of the world, and ignorance of mankind.*
> —JOSEPH ADDISON, STATESMAN AND AUTHOR

But you probably were not even aware you were doing it. At some point most of us have probably done just that. We have unwittingly been conditioned to accept that bias resulting in the practice of that same prejudice. And now we are getting it.

And it is insidious. And it is difficult to prove it is happening. But it is.

Ageism—bias against anyone because of age, young or old in the workplace—is a harsh reality for those favorably disposed to employment as a means of generating income. For the golden generation it is particularly insidious because unlike the young, we will never outgrow it. We will, as a matter of course, face the sting of rejection at the employment office simply because we have gray hair.

The federal government tried to do something about it: Congress passed a law against ageism in 1967 with The Age Discrimination in Employment Act but it affected people who already had a job.

But getting one—well now that's a different matter.

If you are coming out of retirement and your mindset is conditioned to connect in the job market, it may be rough going. Periodically, AARP recommends a few companies that employ members of the golden generation but there are millions of us and so few of them (the jobs)... and don't forget, we're talking dream following here.

If you intend to go back to work in expectation of securing an executive level or skilled level position, getting the position that you feel quite suited for can be a distraction to your new reality when a 30-something man/child gives you a quick review and dismisses you with "We'll get back to you if something opens."

That, dear reader, is a reality check. It is the glass wall, a structure very similar to the glass ceiling except that those who are under the ceiling are often behind the wall.

There is an irony to this. Andrea Coombes of *Market Watch*, writing a piece on ageism, quoted an expert on the subject. "The concept that you can't teach old dogs new tricks is total nonsense," said Paul Boymel, an attorney in the Equal Employment Opportunity Commission's office of legal counsel.

"Every study has shown that, at least where heavy manual labor is not involved, older workers outperform younger workers as a class, with far less absenteeism, far less hopping from job to job, better work ethics," he said, "but not everybody's gotten that message."

Since everybody doesn't know how good you are, one way to deal with the glass wall is simple enough—walk away from it. Yes, walk away from it if you have the legs to do so but sadly, many cannot. Hopefully this is not you.

Innately, many people are employee-oriented and sadly they may have to accept such passive treatment at the glass wall.

When this reality comes to light along with its cruel impact, some folks might feel like saying "woe is me," wring their hands and resign themselves to a wave of futility with a sigh that there is no way out of their situation.

Some may persist and connect with a decent job but most will not and those who do not, may have to make ends meet flipping burgers or packing groceries—oh yes, the employment door at the side of the glass wall is often open for those poverty-wage jobs.

Eventually, those who settle for poverty wages may experience a life of dreariness and despondency. It will be an extremely difficult time for those who are so disposed.

But there are others who know there is a better way. A few will have a clear cut idea on how they will cope and move forward. Their luck is with them.

Others know that there is a better way but they are less certain. But remembering that it is often said that luck is merely being prepared for opportunity, they would like to make that preparation. They would like to move in a direction that would not only sustain them but provide them with the fulfillment that has eluded them most of their lives.

But they are not quite sure in which direction to go.

If that's you, you are not alone. You are in good company and at a good time, too. Great change is at hand. You are going to find out that you may be better prepared than you think.

You may be luckier than you know.

What we call luck is the inner man externalized.
We make things happen to us.
—ROBERTSON DAVIES, CANADIAN AUTHOR

T h o u g h t s

1. An Associated Press article written by David Carry reported in 2004 that some researchers believe that ageism, in the form of negative stereotypes, directly affects longevity. In a study published by the American Psychological Association, Yale School of Public Health professor Becca Levy and her colleagues concluded that old people with positive perceptions of aging lived

an average of 7.5 years longer than those with negative images of growing older. There is power in positive thinking.

2. The largest bias in the U. S. is against the golden generation. The golden rule is not practiced by the younger generation.

3. Bias is based on ignorance. To overcome it a huge educational process would have to be enacted. You don't have the time so if you want to start a new career don't try. Walk away from it if you are able.

4. When encountering bias, do not think ill of the person for his ignorance. That would be negative thinking that you would allow into your subconscious. Wish him well, understanding that his thinking has been victimized and you will be better for it.

5. For every action there is a reaction. When encountering bias, overt or covert, if seeking employment, allow your reaction to direct you to control your life. A career of gold can free you from any bias that would restrict your livelihood.

CHAPTER 3

CHANGE IS EVERYWHERE
CAPITALIZE ON IT

When General Cornwallis had to throw in the towel at Yorktown at the end of the American Revolution, he was unable to face General George Washington or General Rochembeau, his French ally, to offer his sword of surrender. Instead, Cornwallis sent his aide General O'Hara to make the offer.

General Cornwallis had great difficulty adjusting to change that day. Reflecting that change was the tune *The World Turned Upside Down,* the British fife and drum corps played that day as the British troops marched out in defeat amid the formation of Continental and French troops.

The world as the British saw it was indeed turned upside down. The greatest army in the world had been defeated by a ragged lot of farmers.

Not so, however, with the Continental troops—the ragged farmers—who were looking on at the British distress for they saw something else and that was opportunity. They saw it, seized it and formed a new nation.

Opportunity, opportunity, opportunity. It is everywhere. It always is in times of change. When change occurs, seize the moment and the opportunity. It will be all around you.

And that moment in time is now. Great change is underway, change of tidal wave proportions.

So turn your back on the prejudice out there and let the young 30-somethings learn the hard way.

But for us, time is not what it used to be. It is not to be wasted. When we were young, time seemed to be endless. It doesn't seem to be that way anymore, does it?

It is to be valued.

So if you have been facing the greatest bias in the American culture, you might do well to turn your back on it and move forward into the fastest growing segment of American business: self-employment.

If you wish to make a living that you enjoy, earn money and have fun doing it, you are living in the most opportune time in history. There are no social barriers or restrictions to inhibit your attitude.

The legal restrictions in place are to protect you, not prevent you, from moving forward and best of all, the nation and the world are in an incredible state of change and in change there is always opportunity.

In just about every field, new products—not even thought of a decade ago—are now part of our culture and everyday life.

Change is the one constant factor that never changes. We, as a composite of blood and protoplasm, undergo bodily change constantly. Our brain cells die and more are born, fatty cells increase and decrease depending on diet and exercise and our hair thins out, muscles build up and wrinkles show up to name a few dynamics we experience.

And not the least of all, our brain keeps going, dreaming up new things and new ways to make use of those things, including ways to market them.

> *When you're through changing,*
> *you're through.*
> —BRUCE BARTON

The dynamics of change are so fast moving now that opportunity seems to be everywhere. The technologically-attuned find it in technology of course. Those otherwise attuned can find it in information.

Yes, in this fast moving world the need for results has stepped up several paces. People no longer are willing to wait for answers. They want them now.

The attention span, first cousin to patience, has been altered by technology such as television and web surfing.

Ted Selker, an expert in the online equivalent of body language at M.I.T., said in an interview with the British Broadcasting Corporation that the addictive nature of web browsing can leave you with an attention span of nine seconds—the same as a goldfish.

"With literally millions of websites at our fingertips, the attention span of the average web surfer is measured in seconds. If we spend our time flitting from one thing to another on the web, we can get into a habit of not concentrating," Selker concluded.

Think about it. How has your life changed in the past decade? What are you doing now as a matter of course that you were not doing 10 years ago?

Going to the ATM machine, sitting at the computer and talking on your cell phone are three good bets.

Think about the impact just one of those changes has had on your life. You can be assured that there will be other things happening in greater number as the years unfold.

And think also of that goldfish-like attention span. If you stop, yes, stop for a few moments and think about how to attract attention and hold it for 60 seconds—that's just a minute—you will be on the threshold of great possibilities.

*There is change in all things. You yourself are subject
to continual change and some decay,
and this is common to the entire universe.*
—Marcus Aurelius

You are probably not even aware of the changes in your life but have taken them for granted.

But thousands of people have made a lot of money and found happiness bringing their knowledge to you. The form may be a book, a newsletter, a website, a seminar, all about subjects that interested you and captured your attention.

You are living in a time of great change and that change spells opportunity for you because you are living at a time when the sale of information is at a premium.

And whether you know it or not, you have a mother lode of information that can be commercially marketed to many people. Your knowledge can be turned to pure gold.

No, don't shake your head. You have spent a good part of your life developing skills and knowledge on a variety of subjects. Think about it for a few moments.

Yes, stop for a few moments and think about what you have done.

Have you worked at bookkeeping, typing, designing, editing, carpentry, bricklaying, warehousing and driveway paving? If you have, you have knowledge that has value to others. And there are other skills too, hundreds more that have a value others will pay for.

Change has a considerable psychological impact on the human mind. To the fearful it is threatening because it means that things may get worse. To the hopeful it is encouraging because things may get better. To the confident it is inspiring because the challenge exists to make things better.
—KING WHITNEY JR.

Changes in your life in the last ten years.

Debit bank cards

ATMs

handheld language translators

automobile navigation

Sirius radio

financial calculators

e-books

Internet purchasing

High Definition TV

Ipod Video

cordless phones

TiVo

digital cameras

digital printing

invisible fences

financial calculators

bypass surgery

face transplant

blackberries

iPod Nano

Viagra

Ambien

reality shows

MP3 Players

LCD and plasma televisions

electronic pianos

camcorders

portable DVD players

Internet banking

cell phones

broadband phone service

online newspapers

hybrid automobiles

bloggers

cloned animals

DSL highspeed Internet connection

Ladies professional boxing

Ladies professional basketball league

Biometrics

Genetic screening

Change affecting part or all of the world

Population implosion in Europe

Rampant obesity in Europe

AIDS epidemic

Global warming

Global trading

War with the forces of terrorism

Financial processing

Computer technology

Polar caps melting

More on the way

T h o u g h t s

1. Change means opportunity and opportunity is everywhere. Because of technology, the Internet and wireless communication, the opportunity for self-employment is greater now than ever before.

2. In the last 10 years more changes have occurred than at any other 10 year span in history. Changes are occurring all around you and you are probably not even aware of them.

3. You have accumulated a list of skills most of which you forgot you know. Some of those skills can build you a career of gold. They are in your subconscious. They can be activated to reap the benefits of change.

4. Your subconscious is your personal power plant that can be programmed to energize your efforts.

5. The subconscious can be programmed with your thoughts of your new career. If they are coupled with a firm, positive belief, your subconscious will act on them and help you with your new endeavor.

An unfulfilled vocation drains the color
from a man's entire soul.
—Honore de Balzac

CHAPTER 4

FINDING YOUR
INVENTORY

"Getting to know you, getting to know all about you". If you are thinking of Deborah Kerr when you hear those words, put the image of the beautiful and talented lady aside and start thinking about yourself. It is time, no it is a necessity that you get to know yourself if you are going to succeed in your golden career.

Despite the remarkable breakthroughs in medical imagery, there are recesses in your makeup that have yet to be understood. Sections of your brain have yet to be explored. Scientists are forever testing, checking and probing the labyrinths of the brain and endlessly learning interesting new things about your makeup. But as incomplete as the medical studies are, you do know your feelings. And you certainly know upbeat from down and it is the upbeat that fuels your engine. It is the one that gets you going.

There are factors in your makeup, your genes, your early conditioning, that stir your emotions and excite you in a positive way. Some call those factors gifts bestowed by God or nature, others call them talents built into your genetic structure.

Whatever they are, they make you the unique person you are. They exist in a very real way, and unimpeded, they will be the driving force for your career of gold.

The same man cannot be skilled in everything;
each has his special excellence.
—EURIPIDES

That is our starting point for self-assessment. What do you like doing? What something makes you feel good doing it? Deep down, what is the burning passion in your soul or spirit that would drive you to give up sleep, food, TV and everything short of your first born and one true love. Find that and you have found the mother lode in your golden career.

We will be drilling for that huge vein of excellence that lies somewhere in your makeup and when you find it, you will find the beginning of transformation, re-invention and career-change.

As you start to look at yourself, to examine the feelings you have, you will be setting off on a discovery of the person, the real you, that you may have given up on years ago. This is not an exercise in psychology or any of the sciences, it is simply taking a hard look at yourself to determine what you like to do best and admitting to yourself that you really want to do what God and nature designed you to do when you came to planet Earth.

Since emotion is the driving force that moves us to action, let's look at the various triggers and powers that make up these strong feelings that fuel your existence. It is important that you know yourself, the *you* that does things for whatever reason and the why of it all.

Dennis Myer's Story

Dennis Myers has a Ph.D. and a corporate background that some might envy. He looked into himself, saw the whys of his life and then re-invented himself.

Here is his story as he tells it:

"After the last guest left and all the relatives gave up consoling me, I sat in the family room and took stock of my situation. My three daughters had left the nest and were on their own. I hated my executive position in the corporation where I was employed. My home and surrounding neighborhood was perfectly designed but not to my taste. Finally—I mean very finally—my wife of 31 years was now ashes floating around in the Pacific Ocean three miles off the California coast. Alone in my thoughts of the moment, I knew that it was time for a decision about me instead of my usual self-sacrificing role that had been with me for 54 years.

I had a choice, to either sit in a dark room every night, get drunk and wallow in self-pity or make some changes in my life. I got mad! Mad at myself for the life that I had allowed to happen. It fit everyone else's ideas of what was right and good. My goal became to err on the side of what I wanted and what made me happy. I was going to change the rules!

The decision to change my life rather than stay safe with what I had previously done began a 10-year journey that transformed every aspect of my life. Now with my 10th anniversary of re-invention I know that the journey has just begun and the best is yet to come. I am compelled to tell my story with the hope that I can encourage others to get mad! Hopefully some will get upset enough with the misery they continue to accept as a given that they too will launch a journey of their own. I assure anyone, if I can do it, you can do the same.

Now the secrets! This is the good stuff that advertising execs live for. Special magical steps that anyone can do—a chance to grab the golden ring of success! If you just use the 30-day introductory trial offer, riches will befall you and eternal happiness will rule your life! In fact you have nothing to do and there will be a guarantee that failure will be a thing of the past. Sound good? Well, it doesn't work like that. Here are some of the processes and practices that I used along my travels to re-invention land.

First you say goodbye! This may seem rather flippant when considering such a serious challenge as changing your life, but it is a positive first step. It is critical to your re-invention to dispatch.

In my case I wrote a lengthy letter to my deceased wife. I covered all the good and bad. I said everything that I never had the guts to say, or was just kindly not telling the truth about. Once the letter was written, I put the letter in a container and burned it. With the ashes in tow, I drove to the ocean shore, wrapped a rose around the ashes, and threw the flower and contents as far as I could. [Author's note: Please remember if you use this process that everything be natural and biodegradable. No strings and balloons, please!]

Journaling is essential. You have to start focusing on yourself. Mothers always taught us to worry about everyone else, not ourselves. Re-invention takes shape only when you develop a strong understanding of yourself. I focused on two issues as I pondered my true self. I struggled to determine what my "word in the box" was and where my real passions were hidden.

Critical to my re-invention was settling upon one word that described my true redeeming talent or feature that set me apart from other mortals. This word is the reason for your existence. In my case, I decided it was 'creativity'. Passions are not far behind as important discoveries. After much discussion with mentors and self-evaluation, I arrived at four: teaching, cooking, writing, and re-invention.

Philosopher Kahlil Gibran put it best when he wrote, 'Your reason and your passion are the rudder and the sails of your seafaring soul.' I have just come to realize recently that my journey was guided by the need to be creative and pushed along because of my four passions.

One of the important parts of journaling is crafting a plan—at least for a year, preferably five. A plan is essential. If you don't establish plans, goals, and measurements, you will never hold your feet to the fire of change. To change is to dislike where you are, know yourself, have a vision or direction, and be willing to take a first step—then a second—then a third, etc. Little steps in a planned direction tend to add up to big gains.

So where has this decade-long journey taken me? Consider how re-invention worked for me and it can work for anyone—even yourself.

I try to do something creative every day, no matter how small it might be. I no longer work in corporations. I now teach them using executive coaching and consulting skills. I am writing more every day and am nearing completion of my first book. My kitchen is now remodeled to a professional level so that I can cook for wife, family, friends, and clients. My re-invention is not complete—it is one of my passions. My business is now five years old and due for a tune-up! How about Dr. Dennis, the 'Management Chef'?

As you might be considering the possibilities, let me close by describing my bonus for all this work. My home now is in Laguna Beach, where I had only dreamed about living. Every evening I have a glass of wine and watch the sunset over Catalina Island with my fantasy wife of almost 10 years. I found my true soul mate on this journey of reason and passion! As desperately sad as I was ten years ago, I am now blissfully happy with my new life. What better journey could one have in life but toward a new life with a true love at your side?"

Dennis Myers can be contacted at laguna @cox.net

Thoughts

1. You were meant to do something specific in life. Your genes dictate that. *New Scientist* magazine reported in early 2006 that a specific gene linked to athletic performance has been discovered. The gene comes in two variants. People with one variant are predisposed to become sprinters. Those with the second are more likely to excel in endurance events. That is certainly specific.

2. You write your own destiny. You choose to do or make-do. Your genetic disposition is a starting point if you wish to "do." Follow that and you follow your destiny.

3. If one hand of life is tied, cut it loose with the other so you may write your destiny. You will need it to plan your career of gold.

4. Your career of gold will come one day at a time. If success happened all at once it would be difficult to handle.

5. When you realize your interest and you couple that with your learned skills, you have become well-equipped to take the high road to success. Now as you do that, believe that you can go all the way. You will.

> *Women who are confident of their abilities*
> *are more likely to succeed than those who lack*
> *confidence, even though the latter may be much*
> *more competent and talented and industrious.*
> —Dr. Joyce Brothers

Some Eighty Year Old Winners of a Nobel Prize

Age	Winner	Category/Year	Date of Birth
87	Raymond Davis Jr.	Physics 2002	Oct. 14, 1914
87	Vitaly L. Ginzburg	Physics 2003	Oct. 4, 1916
87	Joseph Rotblat	Peace 1995	Nov. 4, 1908
87	Peyton Rous	Medicine 1966	Oct. 5, 1879
87	Karl von Frisch	Medicine 1973	Nov. 20, 1886
86	Ferdinand Buisson	Peace 1927	Dec. 20, 1841
85	John B. Fenn	Chemistry 2002	June 15, 1917
85	Theodor Mommsen	Literature 1902	Nov. 30, 1817
84	Pyotr Kapitsa	Physics 1978	July 9, 1894
84	William S. Knowles	Chemistry 2001	June 1, 1917

The oldest winner of a Nobel Prize was 88 year old Raymond Davis Jr. of the United States. In 2002, he shared it with two younger men, 78 year old Masatoshi Koshiba of Japan and 71 year old Riccardo Giacconi also of the United States.

CHAPTER 5

YOU ARE WHAT YOU ARE THAT'S VALUE

You are a complex character, you know that. We all are. You are happy one day when a check arrives in the mail, angry the day following when a newspaper article takes a contrary stand to your political beliefs, then you are happy again just because the sky is blue and the sun is shining. Who can explain it? Does it feel as though a network of wires is running through your biology, some ready to burn red hot, some to expand into an ever-widening dark noose ready to strangle you while others glimmer with a gold-like effervescence ready to expand into a radiant glow?

Emotions Make You What You Are

The quality of your mental state depends primarily on your emotions. Life is worth living or ending depending on the ebb and flow of them. Vincent van Gogh cut off his ear as the result of an emotional downswing and later took his life while Edmund

Hillary's positive determination took him to the top of Mount Everest and universal acclaim.

Psychologists and philosophers have long fretted over, and debated and discussed, the makeup of emotions and only lately has technology been able to notice the physical cause of them.

But we certainly know the feel of them, the nice and the nasty. We all have felt the soft passion of love and the wild passion of lust, the elation following a hard fought victory, the joy of a loved one's success, the heat of anger, the darkness of despair, the ripping gnaw of revenge. They are the popular emotions, the ones that come to mind when the word "emotion" is spoken.

Passions are vices or virtues to their highest powers.
—Johann Wolfgang Von Goethe

Then there are those that are very much a part of your life, that lurk and live within your makeup but are less easy to understand. Psychologists might say that there are entanglements of your emotions when the nice and the nasty are intertwined with your decision-making process. Those are the ones you should try to understand as you move into the area of understanding why you did what you did as a life's work when in reality you might have wished to do something else.

So let's take a look at the feelings you get.

Some of your Positive Emotions

Joy, happiness, fulfillment, serenity, interest, satisfaction, confidence, courage, desire, elation, gratitude, honor, hope, love, pride, composure, poise, calmness.

These are the emotions poets write of when they take pen to parchment. Positive emotions express an attempt or an intention to include, to deal with, to express, to take the wide view, and to consider the views of others. Positive emotions drive you to do things. They push you up the hills and mountains to accomplish positive things, small and big.

Some of your Negative emotions.

Frustration, hostility, grief, apathy, guilt, arrogance, envy, jealousy, greed, fear, suspicious nature, inferiority complex, melancholy, resentment, blame, tension, stress, escapism, sloth, laziness, uncontrolled anger, bitterness.

These are the emotions that novelists and playwrights work with best. Shakespeare made a great living with them. Negative emotions, as you have probably noticed, express an attempt, intention or desire to dislike, exclude, avoid, suppress, rationalize, deny, cudgel, batter and brutalize your fellow man. The latter three being rather extreme.

Negative emotions are fueled by an underlying fear of the unknown which is a principal fear we all share. Much of it is fostered by the imagination. You may remember when you were a small child entering your dark room on a stormy night fearing whatever you thought might be hiding under the bed. That fear started early.

We learned early too, that fear of the actions of others was real when the first big bully showed up on our block presenting the first threat of physical encounter.

As you got older and learned to deal with those fears, others arose, those that could have far reaching consequences, not the least being those you learned. You could say that some are more negative than others and some more intense.

Emotions Under Cover

Some emotions are disguised as positive or negative, but really are the opposite of what they pretend to be and this is where some of us took a detour in our lives. We fooled ourselves. We took our eyes off reality and accepted an illusion under the guise of rationalization.

Or maybe we were just afraid to stand tall.

It might sound as though the negative emotions are something to get rid of. It is not that simple.

They serve important functions. Basically they show that there is something one doesn't know and can't deal with. If that becomes motivation that is very useful. If one is always joyful, one might miss noticing things that are wrong.

Deep in our depths there lies a circuitry of negative and positive emotions put in place by God and Mother Nature to safeguard the species.

The negative emotions are repellents, warnings to move away from something or someone. The positive emotions motivate us to move toward a goal. Our problems when we chose the "wrong" career in our earlier years may have stemmed from a system malfunction when the emotions got reversed, screwed up so to speak, and the person (you and me) moved toward a career we didn't really want.

That's one explanation. There are others better left to the medical fraternity, but the cause of our misdirection doesn't matter. What is important is the acceptance of the recognition of that detour you took and the desire to do something about it.

Hidden motives

We saw but did not see because it would have been an inconvenience to react responsibly. Such an example of hidden motive would be a type of pity which appears as genuine concern for others, but which is really taking comfort knowing someone else is worse off than you.

In Westchester County, New York, Manfried, an investment banker, had just received a huge year-end bonus. His friend Larry, an engineer for a major automobile manufacturer who was a decade older than he, had just been laid off due to what Larry thought was age discrimination.

Manfried visited Larry on New Year's Day to wish him well and to commiserate. When Manfried left the dejected Larry, he felt sorry for him but at the same time he felt a greater feeling of warmth and security not only for his increased wealth but for his relative youth.

There is also a covert hostility that masquerades as friendliness, which can often be difficult to assess at first.

Jeffrey, a merchandise manager in a synthetic fiber company in New York City, was having difficulty meeting his goals for the year. His anxieties simmered below the surface. Fred, the sales manager, invited him to lunch during which time Fred extended a warm hand to Jeffrey, a few more glasses of wine and some friendly collegial inquiries about the state of business. After the third glass of wine, Jeffrey confided to Fred that he was having some difficulty meeting his goals.

A week after the lunch, the word was rampant throughout the firm that the Merchandising Department was having great difficulties and that Fred was being considered for the newly opened position of Marketing VP.

Only when it was too late did Jeffrey learn that the warm friendly hand of collegiality was masking the hot hand of competition.

Likewise, some kinds of anger or fears might look negative, but might really be an honest expression of involvement and caring. It is the undercurrents of emotion that spell the reality such as the relief a parent feels when a lost child is found.

I think we can agree that at some time in our lives we chose a course of action over another because it was easier, less confrontational or less taxing and used a rationale that was more acceptable socially as our excuse. We hid behind a shield of what was socially acceptable rather than stand and do the correct thing. Maybe we were lazy or afraid of being criticized for doing the right thing even though it might have been politically incorrect.

And that correct thing can begin now as it did for Lynn Colwell whose positive emotions drove her to the work she considers most fulfilling.

Here is Lynn Colwell's story as she tells it:

"At the age of 57, I volunteered for the seventh layoff at the telecommunications company for which I worked in corporate communications. My job history was checkered in that I had held a series of jobs in various arenas that interested me. Work for me had never been about the money, but about doing something that interested me at the time. The problem when I left that last company was that I had no idea what I wanted to do. I figured I'd take a little time to think it over. About six weeks after the layoff I received a letter telling me that because our company had been affected by NAFTA [North American Free Trade Act], I could take advantage of up to two years of retraining. I had always considered in the back of my mind the idea of being a counselor or therapist, so I went back to school to get my master's. But very soon after entering school I realized that at this stage of my life I wanted and needed more than counseling had to offer. After one year, I left school. Very soon after, I awoke one night, sat up in bed and gave my husband a little push. I knew what I wanted to do—become a life coach.

I took about 70 hours of classes and began coaching. Of all the careers I've had, this one best pulls together my abilities, strengths and desires. I am privileged to make a difference in people's lives. And I don't even have to leave home to do it because I coach only over the phone. My e-zine allows me to speak to people in a very personal way, using my experience and life as a way to help them with their own. I have been able to incorporate my core beliefs into my business. For instance, I believe everyone could benefit from a coach some time in her or his life, so I have made coaching affordable. I'm also developing a series of inspirational videos which I will market as part of my coaching business.

I could never have imagined when I volunteered for that layoff that what lay ahead was an exciting and fulfilling career." Lynn Colwell can be contacted at lhcolwell@comcast.net. Her website is *www.bloomngrow.net*

If you want to understand today,
you have to search yesterday.
—PEARL S. BUCK

Man is made or unmade by himself. By the right
choice he ascends. As a being of power, intelligence,
and love, and the lord of his own thoughts,
he holds the key to every situation.
—JAMES ALLEN

Thoughts

1. Your positive emotions are the driving forces that will propel you to success in your career of gold. Your negative forces will offer obstacles which you must hurdle. Protect your positive emotions. Do not allow negative thinking to get in their way.

2. If you allow your passion to be stirred, you may achieve great things in your career of gold. A great feeling of well-being in business is to be financially successful in benefitting others.

3. If your career of gold benefits others, your life will make a difference and may open up roads for others to follow. One of the great wonders of life is the compounded effect we have on others.

Each of us makes his own weather,
determines the color of the skies in the
emotional universe which he inhabits.
—FULTON J. SHEEN, CLERGYMAN

CHAPTER

CLEANING OUT
THE NAY-SAYERS

Conformity is the jailer of freedom
and the enemy of growth.
—JOHN F. KENNEDY

We grew up smothered by the need to conform and to fit into the regimen of whatever authority we fell under—grade school, high school, Brownies, Cub Scouts, Boy Scouts, Girl Scouts, Sunday school, church, temple, mosque, military...the list is endless.

We humans are social beings and our need to collect ourselves into social groups is necessary for the common good. It is an old instinct probably learned when the saber-toothed tigers first had their way with a solitary citizen or two back in *homo erectus* days. But we have progressed. It is no longer the saber-toothed tigers that drive us to collect for the common good. It is us, *homo sapiens,* who does it and for a lot of reasons other than warding off beasts of the field.

Primary among those reasons is efficiency. We experienced it in school when we were told to do this or do that by the teacher. It was never suggested that we do whatever the teacher had in mind the way we thought best. Loss of control would have been the result. It was the way the teacher wanted to run things.

Efficiency

Teach the multitude the elementary needs of life: reading, writing, arithmetic, etc. The nurturing of the individual on a mass basis was impossible for most teachers because they were victims of efficiency, too.

The result, of course, was apathy and dislike by the students. Who wants to sit still when someone else does all the talking all the time—and telling us how to think? The soul and spirit of the student was smothered like a sapling in the shade.

Think back for a moment. How many classes did you look forward to? A few at the most, I am sure.

Of course, some of the saplings made it. Some teachers, like a ray of sunshine streaming through a few dead limbs, brought a spiritual nourishment to a few children encouraging them to grow. But most of us withered spiritually and the talents that God bestowed upon each one of us never found the golden nourishment of the sun upon which to feed.

When we managed to get through grade school and high school we were expected to know what we wanted to be when we got to college, if we did go to college.

Very few of us knew.

As a result, if we went to college, many of us majored in what we thought we wanted or what we thought was in demand by society.

Worse, we pursued what we thought would lead to a well paying job. Little thought was given to the sense of exhilaration, interest and enthusiasm we would feel if we studied a curriculum that would bring delight to our spirit.

Whether we went to college or not, we slipped into corporations and companies, took government jobs or joined the military, all of which were delighted that we were conformed enough to fit right in.

And wherever we went, for every two persons who voiced a word or two of encouragement, there were at least eight nay-sayers who were quick to pitch in with "You can't do that!" "That's impossible!" "You'll never make it!" and "Don't waste your time!"

How often have you heard those horrible words?

Sadly some came from people close to us who had been victims of negativity. Take a look at them and see what they did with their lives.

Knowing them as you do, with their gifts and talents, could they have done something better if they had tried? Probably.

Now take a look at those other faces with the negative voices. Didn't they belong to people who were afraid you might succeed?

Close your eyes and listen for a moment to some of those voices you heard in your lifetime. Probably, the majority of people you know, perhaps 80 percent, had some negative advice for you.

Think about the quality of their voices. Were they warm words? Words of friends who genuinely loved you and hoped for your success? Some perhaps, who had been victimized by the nay-sayers themselves? Most probably were loud, shrill voices of people who viewed you as some form of business or social competitor and were eager to preach their words of doom and gloom.

Pareto Law, the rule developed by Vilfredo Pareto, an Italian economist of the late 1800s is the basis for the Eighty-Twenty Principle. That's the business gauge that 80 percent of the results in company sales are brought about by 20 percent of the people in the sales staff. It is a good gauge for just about everything in the business world.

It works well too, in much of life for the world is driven by a minority of people, the people who ignored those nay-sayers.

They are the ones who thought their ideas were possible and that they could do it and that their time would not be wasted. They went ahead and did what they wanted to do. They are the Twenty Per Centers. The people who make things happen.

You can be one of them.

The Nay-Sayer
Avoid at all cost

- "You just can't do that!"
- "You've got to be kidding. You can't do that."
- "It will never work."
- "Who would buy it?"
- "No."
- "They will laugh at you."
- "You're too old."
- "Don't do it."
- "Oh not again. Another one of your crazy ideas."
- "Be sensible."
- "Look, do what everyone else does."
- "Someone else tried it, a long time ago."
- "Alright but leave me out of it."
- "Oh, come on…"
- "Ohhh… that's too hard…"
- "It's too complicated."
- "Don't waste your time."
- "That's impossible."
- "You're crazy."
- "Learn to settle down."
- "It's over your head."
- "Ohhh… come on. It won't work."
- "I'm telling you now, it will never work."
- "You'll never live it down."

T h o u g h t s

1. Your life is governed by your subconscious. If you allow the nay-sayer entrance, your actions will be affected in a negative way. The words of doom you heard in your early life can create negative behavior patterns in you today resulting in failure and unhappiness.

2. The nay-sayer is a perfidious creature who may rob you of a rich and full life you might otherwise enjoy. To purge yourself of the words of doom and create good habits and a more productive life use autosuggestion.

3. Autosuggestion is telling the conscious mind positive truths which it will pass on to the subconscious mind. This is done repeatedly using such phrases as, "I can do," "I will succeed," and "I am smart."

4. The subconscious mind offers no resistance. Whatever your conscious mind accepts as true, your subconscious mind will readily accept and work to make it happen.

5. Think good things and good things will follow. Think bad things and they too will follow.

CHAPTER 7

JOINING THE GOLDEN GROUP...
THE TWENTY PER CENTERS

When Ulysses S. Grant was a general during the Civil War, he had the unique skill of knowing where his troops and weaponry were at any given time. If the Confederate forces launched an early morning attack on his troops he, upon springing from his cot, would know where everything was and could give instant, and often, effective orders to his subordinates.

His subconscious was called into action when he was, and he was able to issue, with great confidence, the necessary orders for his troops. Interestingly, Grant wrote in his memoirs that before the Civil War he had trouble finding his papers unless they were in a pocket in his coat.

How he went from that mental disarray to one of great precision illustrates the remarkable malleability of the human mind. It also illustrates the power of the subconscious.

Just what is the subconscious? It has been likened to the soul, the spirit, life force and magic power. Whether it is any of those remains a matter of speculation but for want of another term, it definitely is the place where memory is stored. How you tap into it is of vital importance because in addition to being your warehouse of knowledge, it is also the power plant for everything you do.

The conscious mind, psychologists say, is the entry point to the mind. It is the place where rationality occurs and decisions are made. Once the decision or rationality is made and accepted as true, it is then registered in the storehouse of the subconscious. It is where the language you speak is stored for immediate use as well as the road directions to the supermarket. The routines you follow are there, the songs you sing and everything else in life that you use is at the ready.

And very importantly, how you plan your day, how you work your day and how you achieve results from the day are all in the subconscious. It is where your success and your failure is programmed because how you think and work becomes a matter of habit and that habit is registered in your subconscious as well.

And the subconscious, like the computer, doesn't make decisions. It simply does what it is programmed to do.

This is important. Don't miss this. *You are the programmer.*

You can make changes. You will have to because you are about to enter an endeavor with which you may not be familiar and you may experience uncertainty.

Remember all those words from the Voice of Doom, the negative advice from the nay-sayers. Those words are down there, in your subconscious. When you heard them you listened to them and if you followed the negative advice, your subconscious accepted it as the truth. It became part of your program.

Those horrible negative words may be the dominant form of advice that you received. Remember again the 80–20 principle. Most of the voluntary advice you got in life was probably discouraging.

Those negative words probably will provide you with resistance. They will be an urge to resist taking positive action. You have to fight them off.

And you can do it with autosuggestion, the practice of suggesting something specific and definite to yourself. It works against uncertainty and fear very well. Every coach, counselor and platoon sergeant knows this.

Now you do, too.

And how do you use it?

Carefully. Autosuggestion can be harmful.

Rosemarie, a young attorney, was asked to give a speech before a group of schoolteachers. It was early in her career and she was unaccustomed to public speaking but she accepted and after so doing began to have doubts. Fear crept in. "I will never remember my words. My mind will go blank. I just know it. I should never have accepted the engagement." She kept telling herself those things and, of course, her subconscious, being programmed, delivered. Her mind went blank and she forgot her words.

Realizing the power of her negativity, Rosemarie countered it with positive autosuggestion. For a month, each night and first thing each morning, while her body and mind were relaxed and most receptive, she voiced a mantra-like phrase extolling her own skills and attributes on the podium. Her words, now positive, were, "I have a strong, calm voice. I speak well and I remember with clarity all that I want to say."

Her subconscious got the message.

At her next speaking engagement at a service organization several months later, she received an ovation and was booked by the organization to speak again the following year.

When used positively, autosuggestion can deliver the goods. It can be very potent. It can be a great friend.

Now remember again, the 80–20 principle. You have to counter the bad stuff and make the positive advice the dominant factor.

When you decide what you want to do, describe your goal and verbalize it in the present tense—as Rosemarie did—and then gently and repeatedly, almost prayer-like, say it again and again and again. Psychologists say that bedtime and early morning are the best times. Do this every day. Yes, every day for about five minutes when you go to bed and when you wake up.

You will awaken a force within you, resistance will crumble and fear will disappear. You will be on your way to making things happen. You'll be a Twenty Per Center.

Live daringly, boldly, fearlessly. Taste the relish
to be found in competition—in having
put forth the best within you
—HENRY J. KAISER

Thoughts

1. To achieve, acquaint yourself with achievers. They will provide you with positive input for your subconscious. If you want to become an achiever, a Twenty Per Center, start thinking that you can become one. That's the first step.

2. Twenty Per Centers know that the subconscious can be a best friend and are careful to cultivate that best friend.

3. Twenty Per Centers are careful to filter the input into the subconscious mind. They are aware that positive, encouraging input is nutrition for the mind and that the words of doom are like toxic acid.

4. Autosuggestion can be a positive support to counter fear as well as a purgative for the poison of negativity. Use positive autosuggestion each morning when you greet the new day and each evening when retiring. Your life will be the better for it.

5. When it comes to others, words of encouragement go a long way. Be sure to give them to others. Such words may be a factor in another person's success.

Nay-Sayings of Note

"But what…is it good for?"
> —ENGINEER AT THE ADVANCED COMPUTING SYSTEMS DIVISION
> OF IBM, 1968, COMMENTING ON THE MICROCHIP.

"This 'telephone' has too many shortcomings to be seriously considered as a means of communication. The device is inherently of no value to us."
> —WESTERN UNION INTERNAL MEMO, 1876.

"Who the hell wants to hear actors talk?"
> —H. M. WARNER, WARNER BROTHERS, 1927.

"Stocks have reached what looks like a permanently high plateau."
> —IRVING FISHER, PROFESSOR OF ECONOMICS,
> YALE UNIVERSITY, 1929.

"Airplanes are interesting toys but of no military value."
> —MARSHALL FERDINAND FOCH, PROFESSOR OF STRATEGY,
> ECOLE SUPERIEURE DE GUERRE.

"Everything that can be invented has been invented."
> —CHARLES H. DUELL, COMMISSIONER, U.S. OFFICE OF
> PATENTS, 1899.

CHAPTER

TAKING STOCK
OF YOUR ASSETS

Over the course of your work life you have probably done many things and acquired new skills with each endeavor. As is often the case with the acquisition of the new skill, the old one(s) is no longer practiced. To refresh your memory, review the following list of skills and on a sheet of paper, list those you did and are capable of doing.

Abstract skills

Communication skills

Speaking

Writing

Listening and hearing

Verbal expression

Managing group discussion

Negotiating

Interpreting body language

Persuasion

Writing reports

Interviewing

Editing

Forecasting

Creating ideas

Identifying problems

Seeing alternative actions

Identifying resources

Information gathering

Problem solving

Setting goals

Extracting important information

Defining needs

Analyzing facts

Developing

Teaching

Coaching

Counseling

Administrative work skills

Bookkeeping

Budget preparation

Business analysis

Computer skills

Construction

Corel Word

Data Input

Data Mapping

Database administration

Database analysis

Database design

Excel Spreadsheet

Financial reporting

General Ledger

Grant accounting

Grant writing

Graphics software

Injections/Immunizations

Insurance Claims Processing

Inventory Management

Language skills

Macintosh skills

Manuscript preparation

Medicaid administration

Medicare administration

Medical Billing

Medical Records

Medical terminology

Microsoft Word

Sign Language skills

Skilled Nursing Facility

Technical writing

Web design

Soldering

Bricklaying

Interior designing

Marketing

Hair cutting

Hand engraving

Machine engraving

Plastering

Desktop publishing

Coaching

Umpiring

Refereeing

Judging

Now, go over the list. You will be surprised at how much you have come to know. You will discover that you are even better than you thought.

Be sure to take the skills that you have identified and list them on the sheet of paper by your side. If the lists failed to include some skills that you have acquired, add them in.

Now you have your inventory of skills, things that you can do that you can see at a glance. You probably never knew just how valuable a person you are.

These will be the tools—or at least some of them will be the tools—you will use to bring your gold to market.

Now let's find your gold.

T h o u g h t s

1. Your skills are part of who and what you are. Your conscious mind has forgotten all you know but your subconscious remembers everything. Your skills and your interests can be merged into a synergistic energy, a force greater than the sum of your skills and interests.

2. When you couple your skills and interests with the confidence you will develop, you can succeed at whatever you do.

3. If your skills have been dulled by time, you should freshen up on the ones you will use. Do not make the mistake of moving forward thinking you have a sharp blade in your hand when all you have is a rusty butter knife.

4. A skill develops with use and shows itself more with every new assignment and that sometimes leads to new areas of development. This is called growth and is the hallmark of a successful person.

Most people live, whether physically, intellectually, or morally, in a very restricted circle of their potential being. They *make use* of a very small portion of their possible consciousness, and of their soul's resources in general, much like a man who, out of his whole bodily organism, should get into a habit of using and moving only his little finger. Great emergencies and crises show us how much greater our vital resources are than we had supposed.

—From *The Letters of William James* (1920)
To W. Lutoslawski, May 6, 1906.

CHAPTER 9

DOING WHAT YOU DO BEST

What are gifts?

Contemporary psychologists often use the terms talents and gifts interchangeably for those attributes that you are now seeking to unearth.

For our purposes, it is a matter of degree. Leonardo da Vinci, Michaleangelo, Beethoven, Mozart and the pantheon of geniuses we have come to know had creative gifts. They were cultural giants whose gifts allowed them to contribute to Western culture in a manner that not only dominated their time but also transcended time and space because of the influence they had on their art forms and our culture. The probability is if you have a gift, you are well aware of it and you are refining it. If you have not been able to financially benefit from it, the next chapters may help you.

And talents?

Talent is our term for a gift of lesser degree. It is one that might well be used to describe an actor, actress, singer, artist or athlete. He or she is one who has risen to prominence because of his or her ability to entertain, educate or inspire. Pavarotti, Fred Astaire and Ginger Rogers, Lawrence Olivier and Vivien Leigh, Babe Ruth and Michael Jordan had innovative talent and their contributions to western or certainly American culture dominated the era in which they participated. They were role models for others in their own profession.

Our aptitudes

You and I have aptitudes. We all have aptitudes.

You may have gifts or talents as well, but this book is largely designed for your aptitudes, your genetic dispositions—the things that you like to do and are good at doing.

Now with that point clarified, let's move forward.

You may be well aware of your aptitudes and if you are and you wish to use them to full advantage, push ahead to the next chapter.

If you are not sure, take a look inward…

Think back to your childhood when you were in the first grade. What was it in class that interested you? What was it that made you proud when you brought home your first gold star to show your mother—if indeed you did get a gold star? What did you do to get that gold star?

What did you do when you were not in school? On those days when you were home because you weren't feeling well—or at least your mother thought you weren't feeling well—did you draw pictures? Write poems or stories? Watch television? Listen to the radio? And to what did you read, watch or listen?

You were drawn to something for some reason. It doesn't take much to figure out what that meant.

Your genetic disposition was at work when you did those things, whatever they were.

And if you had been in an influence-free zone you might have spent your life following whatever you were initially attracted to.

But harking back to Daniel Goleman's book *Emotional Intelligence* and his writing on early childhood conditioning, that was not to be.

Your emotional wiring was put in place by your teachers and your mom and dad. They were well-intentioned to be sure but they were imperfect beings like all of us and let's face it, who knew about such things as the physical source of emotions, emotional intelligence and all the rest when you were young?

Your parents and teachers were acting as, end products of, their own early conditioning and emotional wiring.

But here you are in your golden years. It's a new day and the shining sun is rising on your horizon. You can change things or certainly improve upon them. You can rewire your system and one way to do that is by setting up your response system.

You can look back at the things that made your own little world sparkle when you were young. And when you decide what they were, you may get a tingle somewhere when you think about it.

When that happens, you will be on the right track.

Creativity and Innovation

The world is a complicated place and so are you. You may have forgotten what made your life sparkle as a child. The fortunes and misfortunes of life may have dulled your senses, snuffing out any awareness you had of the several aptitudes embedded in your early makeup. And yes, you probably do have several aptitudes and maybe some talents and believe it or not, some or at least one of them falls within the framework of creativity.

No, don't think Leonardo da Vinci. I am not referring to that type of creativity although you could be a latent genius. I am talking improvisation, the soul of commerce.

The business and art worlds revolve around it. Monet, Manet and their contemporaries in Paris certainly proved that to the salons along the Seine and everyday, some upstart is proving that in the business world. Think Henry Ford, Bill Gates and the boys at Google.

Creativity as art or under the guise of improvisation is the underlying force in a host of human activities. Creativity as art enhances the soul of our civilization when it is used to bring music into our spirit, literature to our mind and fine art to our wondering eyes.

Cynthia Riggs found creativity writing murder mystery novels at age 70. She wonders where the creativity comes from. Here is her story as she tells it:

"My poet mother, born and raised on Martha's Vineyard, was 90 years old and living alone when I moved back to the Island to be with her in the late 1980s. Our 250-year-old family home was in bad shape, so we took out a mortgage to pay for repairs and opened the grand old house as a bed and breakfast, catering to poets and writers.

A few months after my mother, an active and vigorous 99, died, a bed and breakfast guest urged me to go back to school for my master's degree. I was 66 at the time and simply laughed. But she insisted that I apply and finally, to shut her up, I did, and was accepted into the Vermont College MFA program in creative writing.

I'd been writing off and on throughout my life, but my career had been as mother of five, magazine editor, and boat captain. I wasn't serious about writing. Yet here I was, committed to going back to school with no idea of what to write. My fellow students, the age of my grandchildren, were working on significant literature.

Over morning coffee, a friend told me, 'Write murder mysteries. That sounds like fun.'

So that's how the Martha's Vineyard mystery series featuring 92-year-old poet Victoria Trumbull had its beginning. Victoria, based on my mother, of course, has lost her driver's license after backing into the Meals on Wheels van. The town's police chief offers to give Victoria a ride any time she needs one, and now the chief is stuck with an ancient sidekick.

St. Martin's Minotaur published the first book in the series in 2001 when I was 70. Since then, Victoria has appeared in five more books. I've completed the seventh book, and am working on the eighth and ninth.

This new career astonishes me. Where did all this creativity come from? Was it churning around in my head for seven decades before emerging in an absurd and bloodthirsty outpouring?

My writing has led to my meeting interesting people I'd never have met otherwise, a weekly television show called 'On Island Writing,' a literary journal founded by my writers' group at the senior center, and my first trip abroad.

All my books are in paperback now, all are in large print, and all are being produced as audio books. I'm not yet making a living with writing alone, but together with the bed and breakfast, still going strong, I pay my bills.

And my guests supply me with more material than I will ever be able to use."

Cynthia Riggs can be reached at: criggs@vineyard.net Her website is: *www.criggs.com*

As innovation brings us new tools and toys to lift life from the tedious and mundane and it reaches into science, medicine, military and commerce as new products are developed and old ones improved upon.

Our civilization works on both creativity and improvisation: it is our everyday lives that work on improvisation.

It is our nature to think up new things to satisfy a need. You do whether you realize it or not.

Peter Drucker wrote in his book *Innovation and Entrepreneurship* that the means by which entrepreneurs exploit change as an opportunity for a different business or a different service is a specific tool of use. It is capable, he says, "of being presented as a discipline, capable of being learned, capable of being practiced."

Have you ever straightened out a paper clip to poke something loose in a narrow crevice? Or used a coin to turn a screw? Simple things, but your mind adjusted to meet a need by improvising with what you had to satisfy that need.

That's how things are developed. Meeting a simple need. The U. S. Patent Office knows this first hand; it issues about 70,000 patents each year. That's roughly 284 per business day. Think about that.

Knowing how to enhance your innovative thinking, to think in the direction that will put your career of gold on the fast track, will be the quickest way to find a fulfillment and a stream of income that will brighten your day.

Your highest degree of achievement usually come from doing what you like to do. You will put more time on your work projects and you will refine the end result. You will do that through the better understanding of your own emotions. Once determined, you will be able to rest in the comfort zone of certainty.

"Emotions," Goleman wrote in *Emotional Intelligence* "are at the center of aptitudes." Stress can overwhelm our ability to think clearly as can the toxic emotions of anger and hate. Conversely, positive emotions can propel us forward, fueling our engines with ardor, confidence and enthusiasm.

And it is the positive emotions upon which you will build your career of gold.

OK, here's where you must do some work.

Have your pencil ready and start writing on a sheet of paper the things you did as a child. What excited you? What brought a feeling to your innards when you had the opportunity to do something?

Was it creative?

When you were given an assignment to write a composition, was it a drag?

Or was it the opportunity to take it to the next level and write a short story as rough as it might be?

Did that tingle of excitement stir you when you went into something more physical like woodshop? Did the adrenaline flow when the saws started sawing and the hammers hammering?

Outside of school, did an empty box outside the neighborhood grocers move you to turn it into a fort or a playhouse?

And when it snowed—if it snowed in your childhood—what did you do?

Build a snowman, igloo or fort?

Ride on it with a sled?

Shovel it to avoid slipping?

What did you like the most about it?

The work effort here in this section stems from the brain. You've got to think about this carefully before you answer. Remember now, your natural aptitudes have been buried under a lifetime of rules, regulations and other people's wants and directions. This is where you dig to find your gold.

Many a man who has known himself at ten forgets
himself utterly between ten and thirty.
—CATHERINE DRINKER BOWEN, AUTHOR

Thoughts

1. If you pursue yourself in earnest, you will catch up eventually. Challenge yourself to be what you are. You will be better at that than anyone else.

2. When you stumble upon yourself in your search, your excitement will pick you up.

3. The person you really are may have been forced into concealment by the nay-sayers and their words of doom. It is time to come out of hiding.

4. Burning curiosity is the hallmark of childhood genius. Remember what you were curious about and you may rekindle the spark.

5. When the spark of interest ignites the flame of passion, the driving force to accomplish great things has been set in motion.

CHAPTER

FINDING YOUR GREATEST VALUE

Each of us has some unique capability waiting for
realization. Every person is valuable in his own
existence, for himself alone… each of us can bring to
fruition these innate, God-given abilities.
—GEORGE H. BENDER, U. S. SENATOR

The primary goal is to find that which awakens the feeling of great zeal within you, a zeal that is fueled by the great desire to excel in competition or at being the best you can possibly be. This will make for the ultimate career because of the sheer enjoyment it will give you. Whatever becomes the passion of your life will have, built into it, the all-important ingredient of perseverance. It will keep you going even when "opposing" forces appear before you.

If deep inside you there is an ember burning, you have a very good idea what you would like to do.

If only cold ashes lie at the bottom of your depths then there is work to do.

Meditation is one way. Finding a quiet place and entering into a deep reflection has worked for many. We usually know what it is that interests us but for whatever reason we put it aside for something more "practical."

If deep reflection does not come easy then there is some digging to do. So let's get to work.

Positive emotions are the key. There are several that apply to all facets of your life but a short list has been comprised of those that would apply to an area of interest and entrepreneurial endeavor that would awaken your passion.

Take a look at the emotions on the following short list and become consciously aware of them. When you think of what you did as a child, were any of those activities driven by these emotions?

Anticipation, Confidence, Desire, Elation, Glee, Gladness

The emotions listed are essential ingredients for excitement, the key element of passion.

Anticipation, looking forward to doing whatever you like doing.

Confidence, the knowledge and the feeling that you will do well without question.

Desire, the anxiety to get to do what you enjoy doing.

Elation, the feeling that comes with the successful completion of a project.

Glee, the feeling that comes from winning a hard won struggle against great odds or competition.

Gladness, the feeling that you are doing what you most enjoy doing.

Now relate these to what you did when you were a child before the conditioning factors of parental and scholastic regimen set in.

Were any of these feelings evident?

You probably know or at least you can remember the pleasant moments of childhood. If you can recollect, you may feel a visceral tingle. If you do, your subconscious may be identifying. Focus on that by letting your mind drift back and relive the memories. It will be a momentary pleasure.

Don't let this moment pass. Stop and relive now.

Now write on your sheet of paper what you were reliving when your subconscious nudged you.

This could be it. But don't stop now. Go on to other memories. If nothing comes to mind, the next paragraph may help. If something seems familiar, focus on it. The stirring in your depths will be like a distant drum beating out a message. Go back and listen to it.

> *One must know oneself. If this does not serve*
> *to discover truth, it at least serves as a rule*
> *of life and there is nothing better.*
> —BLAISE PASCAL, 17TH CENTURY AUTHOR, SCIENTIST

We are all different. We advance in our development at varying times, so go back to the early stages of your reading when you discovered the library. After reading about talking pigs and horses you graduated to human characters and there you may have a clue. What did you reach for? Was it *Anne of Green Gables* or perhaps a story of Joan of Arc, George Washington or Babe Ruth? Was it the beginning of a trail of books that had a common denominator, perhaps individualism, adventure or problem solving. There was an attraction for a reason.

When I was a child exploration held a fascination for me. I used to listen with anticipation each Saturday morning to a radio program called the *Explorer's Club*. It captured my imagination and awakened the desire within me to trek into far away and hard to get to places. As a result, I always wanted to travel to Timbuktu, the ultimate far-away place. So in my adult years I did travel to Timbuktu, the hard way, overland and by canoe up the River Niger. Just the way it was done on the radio during my childhood years. There was a feeling of completeness to that journey. And great excitement. And there was a strong connection to my childhood.

So think back to what you liked to read. The interests embedded in your genetic disposition will become more obvious. Once you have established what your genetic interests are, work-fun will enter your life. And why not? It will be what you were meant to do in the first place.

But your work now is not finished yet. Once you establish what it is that you like to do, it is important to determine why you like to do it.

Without that knowledge, you may well be digging for fool's gold. So keep digging. You are going to determine something more about yourself. When you do, your world may open up in a way you never before imagined.

Take your pen and start writing on your sheet of paper. List the things you did as a child. Don't rush into it. Think and reflect. What subjects in school perked you up and got you to lean forward? Do you know why?

What did you do after school? Do you know why you did those things?

Turn that sheet of paper over and do some figuring.

Draw a schematic or a flow chart to give yourself a visualization. It may help. Remember, you are looking for those things that were fueled by positive emotion. The positive emotion is important. That will be the fuel that drives you and you will know when something clicks.

New Wants

When the positive emotion clicks, go to the next step and pencil in what you have learned to want during your adult life. Have you come to want any of the following things regarded as being important in our culture: fame, money, recognition, stature?

These are things our culture values and it is very likely that some, if not all of them, have made their way into your makeup. We'll look at them next.

Over the course of your adult life you have been inundated with a cultural bombardment of the value of celebrity, money and recognition.

The realization of all these factors may come to be as a possible result of your career of gold development. And you may have to deal with them whether you value them or not.

But if you do want them as a definite factor for your life then include them in the suggested layout that follows.

Remember now, you are looking for the emotional base that drove your interests as a child, the interests that reflect your natural aptitudes. If you had more than one significant interest as a child, include them and look for the connecting emotions.

Work out some of those schematics until something clicks. Don't forget, the key element is to discover why you liked doing particular things.

Once you decide what the childhood factors are, do the honest assessment of your current makeup and determine what your social needs are: fame, money, recognition.

By the way, don't hesitate to include recognition: it is a natural thing in all if us and we as individuals yearn to be acknowledged as such. It is natural to want to feel important, so don't hesitate to put that in your current profile. Put self-imposed modesty aside.

Now go back to the review sheet where you wrote the skills you have acquired over the years. These are the tools that you have at the ready.

You now have a good idea as to what you would like to do, your main interest, and what skills you have that will enable you to achieve your goal. You may not use all of them, but you know, in your mind, what your capabilities are.

Jacqueline Marcell, a 55-year-old resident of Irvine, California, has to deal with recognition, even celebrity status. As a result of overwhelming difficulties, she redirected her life and became a best selling author and her book was endorsed by more than 50 authors and celebrities.

She is a former television executive, and author of *Elder Rage*, a Book-of-the-Month Club selection being considered for a feature film.

Here is her story as she tells it:

> "Several years ago, I was so compelled by the heart-wrenching experience of being the sole caregiver to my challenging elderly father and sweet but ailing mother (both with the beginning of Alzheimer's which was not properly diagnosed for more than a year), that once I figured it all out medically and behaviorally—I gave up my 15-year stalled career as a television executive to become an advocate for eldercare awareness and reform.

My infuriation with the healthcare system fueled my passion and resulted in a bestselling book, *Elder Rage;* a popular Internet radio program, *Coping With Caregiving;* hundreds of radio and television appearances; widely published articles; key media including CNN twice, *Woman's Day, Prevention,* the cover story of the *AARP Bulletin* (circulation 22 million); writing an elder care blog; and traveling nationally to deliver over 100 keynotes, including my first big break—replacing Maureen Reagan at the Governor's Conference for Women.

I continued to care for my parents long distance, over-seeing their two wonderful live-in caregivers, adult day care, doctors, and every detail of their lives—for several more years. Then, after 60 years of loving each other, my parents passed, just a few months apart. After coordinating two funerals, sorting their belongings and selling their home, just as I was coming to grips with the grief—the day I came home from a highlight of my life—delivering a keynote address to the Florida House of Representatives—my doctor said the suspicious lump I'd found was indeed invasive breast cancer.

Over the next 18 months, I endured numerous complications from chemotherapy, radiation and five surgeries (including hemorrhaging twice, nine days in the hospital and a blood transfusion), but I committed to figuring out a way to turn yet another horrendous experience into something positive. Now my presentations include the importance for caregivers to take very good care of their own health (I pull off my wig to prove the point), and how to embrace gratitude and humor to remain positive to overcome life's inevitable challenges. I have received e-mails from women who went for their mammograms earlier because of me—and their cancer was found much sooner. Several said I probably saved their lives.

Now I am thrilled just to wake up each day, have stopped worrying about the small stuff, and am grateful to be able to continue my missions to help improve our eldercare laws; educate healthcare professionals how to better help the families they work with; provide solutions and hope to families; encourage funding for Alzheimer's and breast cancer research—and bring awareness to the importance of early diagnosis; expose elder abuse, neglect and exploitation; encourage long-term care insurance/planning; and bring attention to the need for funding of adult day services, which was a huge blessing for my parents and me. I've testified before the assistant secretary on Aging and am featured in an upcoming documentary on the subject.

Isn't it interesting that my life's most harrowing experiences have lead me to far greater fulfillment than I could have ever imagined? So the next time life takes you to your knees and nearly destroys you, focus on how you can help to spare someone else from going through what you have. By helping others, you just may discover your own life's greatest passion, purpose and reward."

Jacqueline Marcell may be contacted at *www.elderrage.com*

Skill is the unified force of experience,
intellect and passion in their operation.
—JOHN RUSKIN, AUTHOR, EDUCATOR

In the arena of human life the honors and rewards fall
to those who show their good qualities in action.
—ARISTOTLE

T h o u g h t s

1. Our childhood ended when our curiosity turned to acceptance, the world became smaller and possible things became impossible.

2. Passion is the spark that lights the flame of genius. It is also the spark that ignites the engines that allow ordinary people to do extraordinary things.

3. Acting on what interests us builds a confidence within us, for we are acting on what we know and when we realize we know more than most others on the subject, we begin to realize our true value. When you come to know yourself, know what you must do to be what you really are, then do it.

4. When you have a goal and the means to achieve that goal, you are on the road to fulfillment. When you arrive there, you will find your true self.

5. Recognition is the acknowledgment by your peers that you have made a worthwhile contribution. Money is the necessary reward for your career of gold efforts. Without money, your efforts will diminish because your attention will turn to other things.

The person with a fixed goal, a clear picture of his desire, or an ideal always before him, causes it, through repetition, to be buried deeply in his subconscious mind and is thus enabled, thanks to its generative and sustaining power, to realize his goal in a minimum of time and with a minimum of physical effort. Just pursue the thought unceasingly. Step by step you will achieve realization, for all your faculties and powers become directed to that end.

—CLAUDE M. BRISTOL

CHAPTER 11

TECHNOLOGY TODAY

It smacks of a fool's errand to speak of such a thing as technology today for what is available today may be obsolete when this book is published, but a few words are warranted.

The key to the *Career of Gold* concept is the computer. It is the centerpiece of your operation. That will not change, only its capabilities and perhaps its appearance, but not the essence of what it can do and what it can do is very powerful stuff indeed.

We will focus on just a few of those things, enough things to put together a marketing package for you to put together in various forms, the information that you may wish to market. Those forms will be audio, video, compact discs, downloadable reports and websites. We will also make available to you avenues of support for each endeavor.

In addition to those formats we will focus on some of the marketing techniques that the computer has hyperactivated or spawned. They are high earning practices that are more easily initiated because of the broadcasting power of the Internet.

Technology has become the center of modern life. Like it or not, it has moved into the home, elbowed its way to the center of our living and has connected us all. Some argue that it has isolated us from our neighbors and changed everything from our attention span to our recreational habits. All of that may be true.

What is undisputedly true is the fact that the Internet has connected over a billion people throughout the planet who use it for such things as recreation, research and buying.

Where are these people? Let's take a look at who is surfing where on the Internet.

	Internet usage	Percent of population
Africa	22,737,500	2.5
Asia	364,270,713	9.9
Europe	290,121,957	35.9
Middle East	18,203,500	9.6
North America	225,801,428	68.1
Latin America	79,033,597	14.3
Australia/Oceania	17,690,762	52.9
Total	1,018,057,389	

Source: Internet World Stats at *www.internetstats.com*.

The numbers are based on the populations of 2006. During the preceding years of 2000–2005, the worldwide rate of increase averaged 182 percent, the Middle East and Africa showing the greatest numbers at 454.2 and 403.7 percent respectively.

So there you have it and it won't stop there. Because of your connection to those billion people the carcer of gold is possible.

The world is round and the place which may seem
like the end may also be the beginning.
—Ivy Baker Priest

The Internet makes it cheaper to design products remotely; reduces the need for vast inventories; provides a better means to target, communicate with, and service customers; cuts the costs of delivering many services and entertainment; and helps companies remove layers of bureaucratic fat. How much will all this add up to? Consider the impact in the United States alone: A study I am completing with fellow Brookings Institution scholar Alice Rivlin and a team of researchers from major U. S. universities suggests that within five years, the Internet may save Americans as much as $200 billion annually. In a roughly $10 trillion economy, this 2 percent savings translates into a potential annual productivity improvement of 0.4 percent. Doesn't sound like much? Think again. If cumulated over 10 years, an annual improvement of 0.4 percent would increase the income of the average American by 4 percent, or roughly $1,600—an amount larger than most of the tax-cut plans bandied about during the 2000 U. S. presidential campaign.

—THE INTERNET ECONOMY, ROBERT E. LITAN—AUTHOR.

FOREIGN POLICY. MARCH 2001

CHAPTER

Your Communications Center...The Computer

New beginnings guarantee new endings

Your gold is your information that stimulates you to the point of excitement. It is valuable to many people. You can supply it to them verbally on tapes or CDs, you can write books, put courses together and even make videos. Technology makes it all easy to do and we'll take a look at those in a later chapter.

The connecting link at some point, between you and your customer/client, will be the Internet. It is the important link for you because the communication is cost effective and it allows for interactivity which is the essence of its great power.

There are more than a billion people out there hooked up to a computer and you will focus on helping out a few thousand to meet your purposes. Beyond that there is no limit. So where do you start? The answer of course is at your computer. It will be your connection to the whole, wide world. It will enable you to access just about anything and it will also be your communication center. Through it you will process words, record them and dispatch them.

The computer. Your communications center

To stay current with the fast moving changes of today, you have to position yourself in the center of that change, that's with the computer.

If you are computer savvy and can surf the Internet, you know its great value. If you are just learning or are thinking about it, there is a great, fascinating education in store for you.

But let's put the Internet aside for the moment and look at another aspect of the computer which will be vital to your career, the word processor.

If you can finger-type as with a typewriter, you will be off and running. If you can't yet type, you can use a voice activated program like Dragon® or Via Voice® that allows you to do hands-free typing using only your voice. You can pick one up at your computer supply store or offline for less than $100.

With Dragon® or Via Voice® you simply talk into the microphone and the word processor does its thing. No hand typing.

You must do one or the other, type or speak. No other options.

The processing of words does not stop there. The computer can also be a sound studio for you. Yes, you can record conversations, music and virtually any sound you want to capture.

And video, too. You can actually make your own video clips for presentations.

And how is this done? You may ask, if you are unfamiliar with this technology.

It can be done because of a thing called software.

We will go into all of this a little further on. Yes, it's a great world.

Now, if I am moving too fast and you are computer frightened and have avoided the computer as you would a skunk on a hot summer night, you must get over it. It is normal to be apprehensive when you tackle the computer for the first time.

Judy, a nurse practitioner who became a life coach thought she was staring into an abyss when she sat down before the computer at age 63. "You will get over it and you will learn very quickly," she told me. "When I started to push buttons and the thing didn't explode, it gave me confidence to push ahead."

If you need a helping hand to get over the apprehension, there are programs in the resource section of this book that will help you. Some of them will soothe your fears, others will educate you and take you to a level of expertise that will surprise you.

And if you don't have a computer, you must make the investment. They are not expensive. Your life will change for the better. It is a must do, so you must do it.

Some terms we will be using

Don't bother to memorize them just check back when necessary.

Camcorder

A self-contained video camera and recording device.

CD-R or Compact Disk-Recordable

Refers to computer peripheral disk drives that allow the user to record content on to a blank compact disk.

CD-ROM

Compact Disk-Read Only Memory; an optical disk from which information may be read but not changed.

Download

To transfer to your computer a copy of a file that resides on another computer.

Firewire

A type of cabling for transferring data to and from digital devices at high speed. Also known as IEEE 1394, faster than USB. Can be used on a PC or Mac.

JPEG

Is the acronym for Joint Photographic Experts Group. JPEG is an image compression format used to transfer color photographs and images over computer networks. It is one of the most common way photos are moved over the Web.

MP3

An abbreviation for MPEG-1 Audio Layer-3. It is the standard technology and format for compressing a sound sequence into a very small file (around 12 to 1) while preserving the original level of sound quality when it is played.

MPEG

The acronym for Moving Pictures Expert Group. MPEG is an international standard for video compression and desktop movie presentation. A special viewing application is needed to run MPEG files on your computer.

QuickTime

This is a digital video standard developed for Apple Macintosh computers. Special viewing applications are needed to run QuickTime movies.

Search Engine

This term refers to a program that helps users find information in text-oriented databases.

Streaming

A term used for transmitting audio or video from your website to your viewer. The audio and/or video files are pre-recorded. The system avoids time-consuming downloads.

For the technically oriented among you, when streaming occurs, a small buffer space is created on the user's computer, and your video or audio starts downloading into it. When the buffer quickly fills up the video or audio starts to play. As the file in the buffer is being used up, more of the file is streaming into it. Very little bandwidth is required for streaming.

URL

This is the abbreviation for Uniform Resource Locator, the addressing system used in the World Wide Web and other Internet resources. Simply, it is the website address.

USB cable

Universal Serial Bus. USB is an interface such as a cable that connects a computer and add-on devices such as a camera and a microphone.

Webmaster

This term refers to the person in charge of administrating a website.

The Video clip

When properly used, the video clip can be the most influential image projection on the web and digital photography makes it economically feasible to do so.

Your principal cost would be your camcorder which you can buy at a very reasonable price, many going for just $200–300 and a six foot USB cable or Firewire (IEEE 1394) for about $10. These wires are high speed hook-ups for your camera and computer when you are running your video "shoots" into your computer.

Studies show that memory retention is far greater for a moving image than for a still picture so if you have a camcorder or intend to buy one and would like to put up a video clip just be sure to follow a few simple rules.

If you are doing a "talking head," my friend and colleague David Seeger, a three-time Emmy Award winner, says the final picture will be very small so be sure to shoot at a distance of six feet or less and always shoot straight ahead at the nose, never down because the head will seem too small and never up because you will see too much nostril.

When you are offering visitors to your website the option of viewing video, you'll have to decide which format to support. At the risk of appearing to spout techno-babble, here are a few facts you should know:

Macintosh systems usually support the QuickTime format. Another format gaining in popularity is MPEG.

Digital home satellite systems use MPEG for their encoding because it offers a good combination of high compression and image quality. And it is that compression that is of considerable importance because that is what facilitates the time it takes for the video to download on your site. You will be testing your customer's attention span: Remember the nine second goldfish attention span.

If you decide to use video clips at some point, your viewers must have the appropriate players. Most will, but for the few who do not you should have a link on your site so they may get a free download of file formats that will work for them.

QuickTime—QuickTime players for Windows (both 16- and 32-bit versions) and Macintosh can be obtained from *http://www.apple.com/quicktime/win.html*

MPEG for Windows, use the VMPEG go to *http://www.sfwmd. gov/org/pld/proj/lec2020/vmpeg.htm*

Putting a less than professional video clip on your site can be counter productive. Editing, which is the removal of unwanted material and connecting multiple clips into a single segment, spells the difference between an effective professional looking piece that influences the buyer to take positive action and one that doesn't. Pinnacle is a good software program that can help you edit and you can get it for about $69. The alternative is to have a professional do it for you. Check the resource section in this book for cost effective film editing services. And for a free editing consultation, contact the 20 Per Cent Club at *careerofgold.com.*

The Audio tool

The compact disc has replaced the tape as the medium for communicating your audio message and making one is the proverbial piece of cake.

It is easy to manufacture these days when you have a computer. All you need is a microphone, which you probably got with your computer. If you didn't, you can pick one up for about $20. You also need a DVD-RW Drive, the part of the computer that enables you to record writing and sound on compact discs (CDs). Most new computers have them and if you have an old timer, you can get a DVD-RW drive at a computer supply store for less than $100.

Companies like Sony® have a very inexpensive software package called Sound Forge Audio Studio which costs about $70. Don't let the word package throw you. It is just a disc that you slide into the computer to activate the program. It is your own little sound studio and it comes complete with 1001 sound effects and a book of directions. There are other good ones on the market too but Sound Forge works well for me so I recommend it. For a few dollars more, Sony will provide you with technical support so you can have someone hold your telephone hand as you are getting started. You can buy Sound Forge at *www.sony.com*.

There is also a book on the market that you can get called *Instant Sound Forge* by Jeffrey Fisher. Written for the novice, you can quickly achieve great results by gaining command of the basic recording and editing functions. Other programs of good repute are listed in the resource section as well.

When you get the Sony® you can learn the process very quickly. You can learn enough to record a speech, interview or a dialogue in 30 minutes.

There are a number of things you can do with the system as well and when you start playing with it, you can add a lot of features such as mixing in sound effects and background music to your information programs.

When your business is set up and you need to have the discs replicated, there are firms that will do it inexpensively. Copymasters Replications® in Nyack, NY and National Media Services® in Front Royal, Virginia come to mind. The resource section will have their addresses.

Sony's software is for the PC but if you have a Mac there is a similar program. Check out the Deck 3.5 LE by Bias®. It turns a Mac into a full-fledged recording studio, and you can record up to 12 audio tracks with CD quality. It runs about $70. You can get it at *www.bias.com.*

> *Progress might have been alright once,*
> *but it has gone on too long.*
> —OGDEN NASH

HELP FOR THE WRITER IN YOU

E ven if you are not a writer, read this. Writing or expressing yourself in some form is a key factor in a career of gold. If you cannot write we will deal with that further on, but if you can, you are in the right place.

Half the population wants to be writers and if you're in that half you have picked a good time to go in that direction because the gates through which you must pass are wide open.

It is the classic channel of communication.

If you do want to write books my suggestion is to consider self-publishing which is less onerous than it sounds. I say this only if you consider your book a product rather than a self-applied ego stroke. And before you respond to that, think honestly about the answer.

When I say self-publishing, I don't mean subsidy publishing, which is having a publishing company, for a fee, publish your book and for additional fees, provide various marketing support features. I don't mean that because that type of publishing is more geared to satisfying the author's ego needs or for one who needs a limited number of books. I do not believe for a moment that you can generate a serious income from subsidy publishing.

If you are interested in a writing career, I suggest you avoid subsidy publishing because industry practices severely limit your income and distribution through this type of publishing. Bookstores are reluctant to carry books published by subsidy publishing firms for a number of reasons, chief among them the inability to return unsold books, as is the tradition in the book business.

And then there is the profit. A small royalty fee from the limited marketing sources available to you is hardly a worthwhile return for your efforts.

By self-publishing I mean you are the publisher.

Now don't get excited. To self-publish no longer requires you move your car from the garage. Digital publishing has changed the nature of the business and makes it affordable and practical to do so. The industry is in the process of great change and for you the change is moving in the right direction. There is opportunity everywhere. I mean everywhere.

And part of that opportunity is the help you can get without incurring any significant fees.

Industry gurus like Dan Poynter, Ron Pramschufer, Fern Reiss and Marilyn and Tom Ross have published books that serve as guides for people who are starting up. Everything is explained.

Poynter's book, *The Self-Publishing Manual,* Pramschufer's *Publishing Basics* and Reiss' book, *The Publishing Game,* as well as the Ross' book *Complete Guide to Self-Publishing,* will take you from the first draft to distribution of the finished book. All the specifics are covered. You will come to know everything you have to know and probably things you will never have to use.

After you read them, get Peter Hupalo's book *How To Start & Run a Small Publishing Company.* He goes into the nuts and bolts day-to-day running of a book publishing business.

And just as this book was being prepared *The Midpoint Handbook* appeared. It was put together by Eric Kampmann and the team at Midpoint Trade Books outlining the 7 keys to publishing success. If you decide to self-publish, this book should be read before and after you have read the others. This is a very important book because it was put together by a distributor and his team and getting a distributor will be vital to your success. You will learn the seven things Midpoint and other distributors deem necessary for acceptance. Contact Midpoint for a copy. The address is in the resource section.

So if writing is your dream, read Poynter, Pramschufer, Reiss and Ross. If it is still a go for you, then read Kampmann's and Hupalo's books. Your eyes will be opened and so will the roadway to your writing dream.

And once you are on that roadway, John Kremer's *1001 Ways to Market Your Books,* the promotional bible of the industry, will give you tips and techniques that will clear up the mystery of moving books. Using just five of Kremer's tips a day will go a long way to help move the sales volume of your book.

Writing to Sell What you Write and Sell

Writing, of course, is not limited to books. Writing much shorter pieces are necessary when you market on the Internet. And you will be doing a great deal of that.

You will be writing sales letters to promote your books, courses, seminars and whatever other forms in which your information is packaged. There is a formulaic art to writing them and it is an art form that you can quickly acquire with the right direction.

Because the Internet is a much different medium than anything else, the writing approach is different. Don't forget, the Internet is interactive—you can communicate with your prospects and customers and they can get back to you—and the writing should be done with that in mind.

In mind also should be the manner in which you sell your information. Please be aware that selling is not simply laying out the facts of your product and saying to your customer, "There you have it. Now how many do you want?"

No, it doesn't work that way. Selling is the art of giving your customer what he can use now or thinks he can use in the future.

How is that done?

Call it friendly persuasion or sales psychology. Call them sales secrets, too, if you like but there are a few principles involved so make a note of them. It took me a long while in my sales and business career to learn all of them and to have my subconscious program them in the proper sequence. You won't find some of them in too many textbooks. Jot all of them down.

First and Foremost. Be totally honest about your product and that honesty should include your products limitations. And those limitations should be spelled out up front. Even if it isn't much, mention it.

Once you advise your prospect at the beginning what your product does not or cannot do, she will believe everything else you tell her. She will trust you. Having that trust is the single most important factor in selling or marketing.

It is vitally important that the limitations be spelled out up front because if you wait until the end of the sales letter or sales presentation or whatever sales form you are using, it will appear to be an end-run or a slip-in.

And that is a turn-off.

Second. Be likable. How is that done on the Internet? Connect with your target audience on a commonality. You are one of them. Your target market should recognize you as a member of whatever tribe to which you all belong.

Third. Offer legitimate praise. People know flattery and will brush you off if you use it. If the praise is real, they will know it and love you for it. On the Internet, you will know your target audience. Google or Yahoo will research them for you. Use legit-imate praise based on facts in your sales letter.

Fourth. Reach out. The computer gives you the opportunity to interact. Use it to help individuals in your target audience. Offer help in some way. If you do they will feel the need to recip-rocate. To many this will mean a purchase.

Fifth. Show endorsements. What you say may be convincing. When other say the same thing—people they know or relate to—it is a pronouncement from a disinterested third party. It leads to the close. This is critical.

To put these pearls of wisdom together, and a lot of other things, too, there are gurus who can help you.

Preeminent are marketing heavyweights Dan Kennedy who wrote *The Ultimate Sales Letter: Boost Your Sales With Powerful Sales Letters, Based on Madison Avenue Techniques* and Joe Vitale who offers an Internet course entitled *Hypnotic Writing*. John Caples and Robert Collier have also written books on copy writ-ing and are highly recommended. You will find reference to all of them in the resource section.

Please remember, opportunity is all about you. Not only are the channels for writing wide open but the advice to get your information into those channels is readily available. There are no longer any secrets to the publishing and writing business.

Help and opportunity is everywhere, so if you have always wanted to be a writer like Cynthia Riggs but don't quite know where to start, try one of the recommended books.

And be sure to check out the books on how to write sales letters. It is a specialized art form and you will find that knowing how to write a good sales letter goes a long way when you are marketing on the Internet.

> *The secret of good writing is to say an old thing in a*
> *new way or to say a new thing in an old way*
> —RICHARD HARDING DAVIS

Thoughts

1. Writing will be an essential part of your life, unless, of course, you can't write. Then you'll have to dictate. Either way, you'll have to get the word out.
2. You can write if you have mastered the simple sentence. It's that simple. Just string a few together and you have a paragraph.
3. A paragraph in a sales letter is like a paving block in a garden pathway. One leads you to the next. And that one to the next until you finally reach a particular point where you are resting on a shaded bench convinced somehow that you are fortunate to be in such a lovely place.
4. When writing your sales letter there is no need for art, originality or great prose, just benefits honestly explained in a concise, direct way.

5. The key to writing well is to simplify your writing. Be direct,
    unwavering and precise.

> *To write well, express yourself like common people*
> *but think like a wise man. Or, think as wise men do,*
> *but speak as the common people do.*
>
> —ARISTOTLE

CHAPTER

THE
MARKET

There are always opportunities through which
businessmen can profit handsomely
if they will only recognize and seize them.
—JOHN PAUL GETTY

OK, you're thinking you've got all this technology down pat, what's next? Where do we go from here?

What is the first thing I should do?

Should I write a book on what interests me?

Make a CD?

Have a website designed?

No. Emphatically no, to all the above.

The first thing you do is find your market before you do anything, even before you do a business plan. You must have a target before you start shooting. There are a number of reasons why people will buy your information. Making money, saving money, saving time, increasing safety, ego gratification and curiosity are six of the main reasons and when you look for your market think of any of those six reasons.

Let's start by what you want to do and use a hypothetical case as an example.

Food is a popular item. For the sake of illustration let's suppose that you wanted to channel your love of food into your new career. Dennis Myers redirected his life towards it and so did Jude Wright of Chino Hills, California. Jude, a former office manager, will tell us her story a few pages ahead.

Continuing our hypothetical on the food subject, let's start where all things start, with your thoughts.

Claude Bristol wrote that thought is the original source of all wealth, all success, all material gain, all great discoveries and inventions, and all achievement.

With that thought in mind think well about the next step because it is critical. It will be the road you will take to bring your food information to the world market.

And the first thought you must have is what market exists in a positive state of change that has a highly lucrative base that would meet one of the six criteria.

The lucrative market must exist for you to hit pay dirt. So once you have decided what your area of interest is then you decide what your target will be and that will be the richest section of your general market.

Research will find the opportunity for you.

And that starts with change for that is where the best opportunity lies.

Let's suppose you really are interested in food. Now relative to food, what is changing?

New recipes, of course, are constantly coming to light from all parts of the food world but that's not going to do it. Greater opportunity will lie in greater change. And greater change is happening.

In Europe, the Republic of Ireland has emerged from the modest country it once was to a highly desirable place in which to live and work. Big change there.

The British magazine *The Economist,* in 2005, called Ireland the best place in all the world in which to live. The standard of living is very high and so too, the educational levels. That means the lifestyle is high up there.

Out of that, one form of cooking that comes to mind is new-Irish cuisine. No, not corn beef and cabbage Irish. Old-fashioned stereotypes are out. New-Irish is really continental with an Irish touch and it is starting to get attention. It is starting to be considered *in.* Typical are such tasty items as Mussel Soup with Oatmeal-Herb Crust and Warm Woodland Salad with Champagne Vinaigrette.

You might say it sounds like something you would find in a good restaurant and it is. That's the New-Irish cooking.

And now for the most important factor: Who would be your customers, your market?

Your profitable and lucrative market?

A little research is necessary. Let's take a look. According to the U. S. Census Bureau, there are 34.3 million Irish-Americans in the U. S. Thirty percent of those age 25 years old and older have bachelor's degrees or higher, and their annual median household income is $48,900. For perspective, the U. S., as a whole, has a median income of $42,000, and 24 percent have a bachelor's degree or better.

Those are positive numbers. You are looking at a lot of people who have a lot of money who would be quick to identify with something of value pertaining to their ethnic heritage. That is human nature. That is also ego-gratification.

Because there is a huge Irish-American market, it would be a good way to go since the New-Irish food field is not cluttered now. Checking Google, one can see the beginning of a build-up but most of it pertains to cookbooks, recipes and magazine articles. There is definitely room to ride the crest.

But let's narrow that down. Within that huge market, there are tiers of income. The $48,900 referred to by the Census Bureau is the median income, that's the middle. That means there is a vast number of people making a lot more than the median income. The more money, the more fine dining. There is a very wide target there. This is an opportunity.

You're not Irish you say, you'd rather do Italian because you're Italian. Being Irish or Italian has nothing to do with any of this, but if you love Italian food and that is your food passion then find your niche in the Italian food field. It is fairly cluttered but go for it if it is your passion and ask yourself, does it meet with any one of the six criteria?

Now let's suppose you have a strong entrepreneurial streak and opt for the road of change. Even though you are not Irish you love food.

The next step is to make yourself an expert in New-Irish cooking. You work the recipes, read what books are available and then you proclaim yourself to be an expert. That's how it is done in this fast moving world. It does not require years of study and attendance at a *cordon bleu* school. In the world of public relations and promotion, the word "expert" is self-proclaimed. Like Napoleon, you put the crown on your own head.

> *An expert is someone who knows a little more*
> *than the person who is willing to hire him.*
> —Wolfgang Ryan

Now you can step into the vanguard of a newly developing area. The food is new, or at least, the label New-Irish is new, the market is huge and it is targeted. You know who they are so you can connect directly with Irish-American demographics.

How do you find such demographics?

They are available through such sources as Irish-American newspapers and magazines. Their advertising rate cards will give you a breakdown and at no charge to you. For reference I checked with the *Irish Echo, the* largest Irish-American newspaper in America. The paper claims a circulation of 100,000 with an average readership that is 36 years of age, of which 70 percent are college graduates with an annual income range of $90,000–$120,000.

You are in the money here. You have narrowed down the 34 million to 100,000 as your core target.

And the newspaper has an online edition. There is definitely opportunity there.

We have looked at a hypothetical instance of researching a possible program if food was your interest. If interests other than food stir you to action, you have to do your research with the established criteria of the reasons people would buy your information, coupled with the existence of the target market. Looking back:

- We looked for positive change in lifestyle and saw Ireland.
- What kind of change did we see? Economic upswing. Development of sophisticated New-Irish cooking.
- Where did we see market? Thirty-four million Irish-Americans.
- Does market qualify economically? Yes.
- Core target identified? Yes $90,000–120,000 group.
- Does core target meet one of six criteria? Yes, egogratification.
- Core target accessible? Yes, through newspaper and newspaper's web edition.

OK, now that I'm doing New-Irish cooking and I have a target market, what next?

What is research, but a blind date with knowledge.
—WILLIAM HENRY

Thoughts

1. Research is often a trail that takes us nowhere. But when it does take us somewhere, it is often the beginning of a new opportunity. There is an abundance of resources on the Internet. Research today is easier than at any time in history.

2. Research often takes us past areas others have gone but when you see something others have not, you may have found the very thing that will be your signature.

3. Research can be seductive when it yields interesting but unimportant things because the tempting tidbits of information that distract you, steal from you, your most precious commodity: time. Remember to stay focused.

4. Time gone by can never be recaptured. Lost time equates to one less thing you can accomplish. It is the one unique force in your life that can never be replaced.

What is Marketing?

In plain and simple terms, marketing activities and strategies result in making products available that satisfy customers while making profits for the companies that offer those products. That's it in a nutshell!

Marketing produces a "win-win" because:

• Customers have a product that meets their needs, and

• Healthy profits are achieved for the company. (These profits allow the company to continue to do business in order to meet the needs of future customers.)

Stated another way: A focus on what the customer wants is essential to successful marketing efforts. This customer-orientation must also be balanced with the company's objective of maintaining a profitable volume of sales in order for the company to continue to do business. Marketing is a creative, ever-changing orchestration of all the activities needed to accomplish both of these objectives.

—U. S. SMALL BUSINESS ADMINISTRATION

CHAPTER 15

WHAT'S IN A NAME? EVERYTHING

The image is more than an idea. It is a vortex or
cluster of fused ideas and is endowed with energy.
—EZRA POUND

Your company name is next. Once your area of interest is determined, it should be less about your product but more about an identification with your customer singularly or collectively. This creates a connection with your customer and the members of your target market.

It is a form of bonding and it will register with the members of your market. Relative to the aforementioned New-Irish food hypothetical case, a company name like Celtic Gourmet.com might be more effective than a company name like The New-Irish Food Store.com. If you were an upscale Irish-American who threw dinner parties to what name might you respond?

Don't forget the principle of selling identification. You want to be a member of the tribe.

When you are throwing around some names for consideration, be sure to consider ease of pronunciation and the rhythmic flow of the sound. And when your short list of names is being whittled down, make sure that the final choice doesn't sound like another company's name. If it does, that would mean that there might be a URL (the web address) similar to yours. That, you do not need.

When you are working on your long list be sure to include the emotion factor into the name. When someone sees the name of your company, book, project or whatever, what emotion is stirred?

Think for a moment what happens when you see the name *Overstock.com*. When I see it, the slight stirrings of greed twists in my innards and I immediately think of a very good deal. That's an emotion stirrer that will attract buyers. Be sure to inject an emotional pull into your name.

When you have your short list put together, prioritize them, then start looking in the various corners of the commercial world to see if they are taken. There is no sense rushing a name into use, only to find that someone else has it up in lights.

I've been through this a number of times, here's the way it is. First let's touch on structural issues, then we'll look at the name for the Internet.

The structural or legal issues regarding the selection of a name fall into two basic categories, the government require-ments for registration of business names and the optional ones.

The government requirements are mandatory and begin at the county level, usually the county clerk's office. This is required if you are unincorporated and are functioning under a name other than your own. Sometimes referred to as a "dba" (doing business as), it is required if you are doing business with a name other than your given name. This will protect your created name from being used by anyone else in the county. There is usually a fee of a few dollars.

Please note, there is very little protection here when you are on the Internet but it is a local requirement. If you function under this business format you are personally liable for all the debts of your business.

If you take it a step-up to incorporation or a limited liability corporation you are personally shielded from your company's debts. In the process, when you register your papers with your state's Secretary of State, the process will reveal if someone else is using the name or one similar to it in your state. Once the paper's are filed, the name is yours on the corporate level in the state in which you filed.

One interesting note: If someone is already using your name as a dba, they may continue to use it.

On the national level (which should concern you since you will be national—even international—on the Internet), you should register the name with the U. S. Patent and Trademark Office as a trademark which puts the rest of the country on notice that the name is already taken. You can contact the patent office at *http://www.uspto.gov/.* It will cost you $230 to register online, $289 by mail. Your name is an invaluable asset and you should go to great pains to protect it. If you don't and you are enjoying success, someone could pull it out from under you. Not a good thing to have happen.

The Small Business Administration has a great website at *http://www.sba.gov/hotlist/businessnames.html.* It goes a long way to helping you on the issue of business name selection. Check it out. It has direct connections to every state in the union.

If you are going to incorporate, go to your lawyer if you are uncertain about legal proceedings and if you are comfortable with the process, check out *http://www.corporate.com.* It is a company that has been incorporating people for a very modest sum. They have been around for years.

Now for your name and the Internet.This is a relatively simple process. In order to secure your company name—called a domain name—on the web you must register it for that specific purpose. When you do, if it is not available, you will be told immediately by the registration firm.

There are a number of firms who do this and you will find a host of them on Google or Yahoo. Just punch in "domain name" and you will be overwhelmed by the number of firms that show up.

Securing a domain name can cost as little as a few dollars or for the unwary several dollars, so shop around.

Companies like *iPowerweb.com, GoDaddy.com* and *Register .com* are a few of the many firms that advertise cost-effective service. Check them out and read all the print, large and small.

> *In real life, unlike in Shakespeare, the sweetness*
> *of the rose depends upon the name it bears.*
> *Things are not only what they are. They are, in very*
> *important respects, what they seem to be.*
> —HUBERT HUMPHREY

Thoughts

1. The name of your business can be the first impression a prospect will have of you and first impressions are forever. Don't forget that.
2. A business name should convey a bonding with the target audience. It should symbolize the value system of the people you are targeting.
3. A business on the Internet should promote its product or reason for being in its name for the purpose of branding. When your name is out there it will become synonymous with your prospect's need when that need arises. It is name retention.

Some Interesting Business Names

Leaven and Earth ~ A Bakery in Berkeley, CA

Salt and Battery ~ Fish and Chips, Brisbane, Australia

Citizen Canine ~ Dog Kennel, Oakland, CA

Barking Lot ~ Dog Grooming, Orangeburg, NY

Stir Crazy Café ~ West Nyack, NY

Many Happy Returns Inc. ~ Tax return preparation, NYC

Den of Antiquities ~ Victoria, Australia

A Den of Antiquity ~ Asheville, NC

It's A Crewel World ~ Salem, MA

Wok N Roll ~ Multiple locations across the U.S.

Beach Bum Tanning ~ Paramus, NJ

Eye-Magination Optical ~ Pomona, NY

Hard Wok Cafe ~ New City, NY

Pizza My Heart ~ Santa Cruz, CA

People.delphiforums.com

CHAPTER 16

THE WORLD IS GETTING SMALLER IT IS NOW YOUR OYSTER

But what if food is not your thing; you prefer industry. You want to be a wheeler-dealer. You envy Donald Trump and Martha Stewart. Then you must scratch your head and come up with ideas on how to jump into the wheeler-dealer business. So you, wisely, look for change.

Arguably the biggest change in business today is globalization. It is a virtual juggernaut that is changing the face of trade and companies, major and mid-size, are jumping into it.

In its 9th Annual Global CEO Survey, Price Waterhouse Coopers, the international business consulting firm, wrote that it is unstoppable. Companies are embracing globalization to gain new customers and access new markets.

Based on interviews with 1,410 CEOs worldwide, the survey concluded that globalization is a positive force and contrary to popular perception, the primary driving force is market development, not the securement of lower cost goods which is actually second in consideration.

The principal target are the BRICs (Brazil, Russia, India, China) with China getting the most attention and India and Brazil almost tied for second.

Let's explore an idea and see if it fits with something that would stir your high-flying soul.

Thinking change, look at the biggest target of all, China.

China is emerging as an economic power because of its low-cost manufacturing facilities. If you would like to be that international businessman or woman, how about compiling a directory of Chinese manufacturing facilities and selling it to small business people who are looking for that edge? Or perhaps represent some of those companies here in the U. S.

What can it lead to? The possibilities are endless. It could be the beginning of a reverse list: companies in China that would buy from companies in the West. But whatever you do, if you decide something like this, know and/or study the market first, then service it with the Chinese imports. A project like this can lead to anything. Motion attracts interest.

Now, how do you find the Chinese sources? Here's how.

Go to the website of the Embassy of the People's Republic of China in the United States at *http://www.china-embassy.org/eng/*

That's the easy part. Now follow this trail:

1. When the homepage opens press Economy or Trade in the left column.

2. Press Economic and Commercial Section of the Embassy.

3. Press *http-://U.S.mofcom.gov.ca.*

4. Press English Version.

5. Go down to the very bottom of the page and in tiny letters you will see Bizmatching. Press that.

6. You will then find a way to connect with manufacturers in a wide variety of industries. You will be provided with the means of contacting them.

If the possibilities in China interest you, the opportunities in India will make your eyes boggle.

India is emerging because of its technological expertise and its servicing with that expertise as the outsource destination for many western nations. Before I delve into that, here's what Price Waterhouse Cooper® says about India:

"India's economy is sizzling and is one of the fastest growing economies in the world. This rapid development has created, and will continue to create, improved demands for additional sources of capital and investment opportunities from potential foreign investors. India is devoted to implementing fully economic reforms, encouraging foreign investments and technology inflows to create a global powerhouse."

There is tremendous opportunity there for two reasons. India is technologically advanced so the trade people have collectively gathered starting points which are the associations of companies, the sources of product and service. It is excellent and is readily available. But here is where the real opportunity lies: India is huge. It is the second largest country in the world and because of that there is no central source of company categories. The Indian National Trade and Industry Association will give you entry to the associations. You can compile from there.

The companies of your interest can be located by specialization so your research can be focused. Take a look on this website for the National and Trade and Industry Association of India, *www.indiaonestop.com/listingstrade&industryassociations.htm.*

If you enjoy organized research you can find a veritable bonanza here.

There are literally thousands of businesses in China and India, two countries that are supplying low-cost goods and services to the West.

And what about Brazil, almost tied with India for a close second behind China? Emphasis is being placed on scientific research in Brazil with 60,000 scientists in residence… and you know what research produces. There is great opportunity there and the trade relations between the U. S. and Brazil is good. It is reflected on the website of the Brazilian-American Chamber of commerce at *www.brazilcham.com.* It is easy to navigate. More ideas there and a host of businesses.

Large corporations in the U. S. may be privy to some of the companies in those three countries but what about the small Western companies? Everyone is interested in buying low and selling high. That is always a good starting point. Knowing where to buy low has to spark interest in anyone with any business savvy. Lists of low cost companies have value.

But I repeat again, know your market first, do your research and identify it. Then service it with the information you can organize.

Contacting various consulates and embassies could go a long way toward securing a list of companies providing those goods and services. That list could certainly be of value right here. Many, I suspect, would pay for such information and quite well, too. Just an idea.

Motion creates interest and it starts with your thoughts of looking for change.

Research serves to make building stones
out of stumbling blocks.
—ARTHUR LITTLE

Trade is the natural enemy of all violent passions.
Trade loves moderation, delights in compromise, and
is most careful to avoid anger. It is patient, supple, and
insinuating, only resorting to extreme measures in
cases of absolute necessity. Trade makes men
independent of one another and gives them a high
idea of their personal importance: it leads them to
want to manage their own affairs and teaches them to
succeed therein. Hence it makes them inclined to
liberty but disinclined to revolution.
—ALEXIS DE TOCQUEVILLE

Finding Change

Change is all around you. You can find it in a variety of ways. One way is to listen to the professional forecasters. The editors of *The Futurist*, the official magazine of The Futurist Society, quali-fies. Over the years they have predicted such things as the Internet, virtual reality and the end of the Cold War.

Their call for the year 2006 includes such things as the rapid growth of wind and tidal power in the next five years, the consid-erable rise of science and engineering research in Latin America, and a job boom in the next decade for solar industries. A sub-scription to *The Futurist* might be a good idea.

Some other suggestions:

1. Join associations of your special area of interest. You can find them in the *Encyclopedia of Associations* in your library. It is published by Gale Research.

2. Read government publications for industry specific infor-mation.

3. Check with foreign embassies and consulates.

4. Consult the government data website *www.thedataweb.org.*

5. In your area of interest, contact manufacturers and distribu-tors to determine what their needs are. What is it they would like to have?

6. Read journals and magazines that deal with small-business or business in general.

7. Subscribe to magazines like *New Scientist* and *The Futurist* or read them in your library's reading room.

8. Attend shows and conventions. Pick up brochures and catalogues of the attendees.

9. Study the U. S. Census figures and the Consumer Price Index.

10. Frequently check the best seller lists for non-fiction books that are moving. Examine them from different angles for possible inclusion in your area of interest.

The mark of the man of the world is absence of
pretension. He does not make a speech; he takes a low
business-tone, avoids all brag, is nobody, dresses
plainly, promises not at all, performs much, speaks in
monosyllables, hugs his fact. He calls his employment
by its lowest name, and so takes from evil tongues
their sharpest weapon. His conversation clings
to the weather and the news, yet he allows himself to
be surprised into thought, and the unlocking
of his learning and philosophy.

—RALPH WALDO EMMERSON

Thoughts

1. Observe constantly that all things take place by change. Condition yourself to accept that fact and that change is the natural order of the universe. It happens in the U.S., Europe, Asia and every place in existence. The amount of opportunity in the world is enormous.

2. When you are establishing your business, factor into it the element of change. New products, new sales material, new marketing techniques. Change should be a constant factor in your business.

3. Technology in Asia and South America will be bringing change to services and methods in Europe and North America. The vigilant eye cast in the direction of those areas will reap huge rewards.

CHAPTER 17

YOUR PRODUCT
AND PROGRAM

You have done your research. You know your subject, after all
you are an expert in the field, and now you want to start
shaping things up and costing things out.

You have decided on a multi-media package because it lends
itself to your subject. But can you afford it?

Most likely. If the term multi-media sounds heavy, it is not, I
can assure you. It lends itself to every subject and the various
components are not expensive. You can get your products and
business started for less than $700.

OK. What is multi-media? It is a collection of different
forms of expression. That's all it is. For your initial purposes, it
will be a website, and possibly a CD, an audio disc, downloadable reports or downloadable sound and it could include a
book or a downloadable e-book. And it could also include
something as simple as reports consisting of several sheets of

paper containing information. As you develop your business you could also have video presentations which sound more expensive to produce than they are. That's about it.

Let's look at them individually.

The website is the cornerstone of your business. If you have a flair for technology and/or art you might be able to do it yourself using one of many software packages available. There are several that provide templates and miscellaneous services, including hosting. Two such companies are Homestead Inc. at *www.homestead.com* and Yahoo SBS at *smallbusiness.yahoo.com*.

If the idea of doing it yourself has little appeal, scout around for a cost-effective designer. You will be surprised at how reasonable some of them are. Check the resource section in the back of the book. We have listed some we consider to be excellent.

Check in with Website designers and the others for specifics and a look-see at their portfolios.

Peripheral costs to the fee of the designer would be a charge to have your website hosted (think of a building and you as a tenant), the annual fee for the domain name and if you are going to process credit cards on your website (which you should), a small initial set-up charge and then a per unit charge for each sale. Your web designer can help you with all these.

If you would prefer a turnkey package of website design and marketing package, go to the 20 Per Cent Club *www.career ofgold.com*.

After your website is designed and running, you will use it to deliver your message to the world. It will not only convey your message but it will serve as an access for your customer to engage your service or information.

Autoresponder—The cornerstone in Internet marketing is the autoresponder. It responds to your customer when he or she buys your product with a thank you message. It also records their name and e-mail address and it literally converts your visitors to subscribers. By sending your subscriber base periodical e-letters of information and opportunities, you can convert many of your subscribers to buyers.

The autoresponder enables you to build your mailing list, deliver your newsletters and track your results while you are doing other things.

Downloadable reports—There are no production costs in downloadable reports other than the time you put in writing them. This is virtually pure profit. You write the report or information on your Microsoft Word or Corel Word program and convert it to PDF format.

This conversion to PDF format is necessary since PDF (Portable Document Format) can be opened by anyone. Your particular word processing program is not always in sync with everyone else's program. PDF resolves that problem.

By the way, when I write of PDF format, think shape and neutralization. Your document is reshaped to page size and it is reformatted to "neutral" so it can appear on anyone's computer no matter what program he or she might have. A Macintosh does not normally open a PC file and vice versa. With PDF it can.

Your computer may not have come with PDF. Many do not, so if you don't have it on your computer, get it. You can buy it from Adobe at *www.Adobe.com* or get PDF converter free from a company like Primo PDF at *www.primopdf.com*.

The person receiving the e-book must have Adobe Reader which can be downloaded free from *www.adobe.com*.

For your customer's ease, you can set up a link right to it. Now when your customer pays for the report with a credit card, the customer will be sure to get his or her report without any problem.

The CD-ROM—Compact Disc-Read-Only Memory. This is your information on a compact disc. It can hold up to 300,000 pages of text. These are "typed" on your word processor the same as the downloadable file and then burned onto the disc in your DVD-RW drive.

There are production and mailing costs which increase the cost to the customer so the information should be more extensive than that which is downloaded. With a DVD-RW drive you can make the basic CD for the cost of the disc which is less than $1 and duplication companies like National Media will crank out any number from 1 to 1000+.

When duplicated, the media company will stamp out the disc which means the viewer can only read it and cannot add any additional data.

In quantities of 100 the published price ranges from less than $1 per unit to less than $2, depending on the desired imprint on the disc itself.

There are people who prefer CD to downloading for a few reasons, one being the psychological feel of getting something tangible for their money.

Audio disc—This is a CD-ROM with sound and that sound can be anything that might interest your customer. It can be you or some distinguished person doing a seminar, reciting a story or a series of stories relative to your interest. An interview of a dignitary relative to your interest is always an item of interest. Anything that might interest your customer as she drives up the parkway.

Audios are made with a software like Sony Sound Forge® or Freeverse's Sound Studio 3® for the Macintosh and are very cost effective. They can be downloaded, played on a speaker that your web designer can build into your site or sold as a CD with costs very similar to a text CD.

E-Book—This is a downloadable book. Usually shorter that a paper book, it is a book, ideally, of about 100 pages or less. It can be more but in recognition of today's fast moving pace, people want their information fast, not only in delivery but in compact, easy-to-read form.

You can type out your e-book on your word processor and format it yourself with PDF.

A cover for an e-book is important because image sells. It is what makes an immediate impression on the mind and stirs interest. Your web designer might do it for you. If not, contact The 20 Per Cent Club. It will do it for you for $20. Go to *www.careerofgold.com.*

The cost for the e-book can be as little as the cost of the cover—and your time, if you write it yourself.

Book—A print book is a great credential, perhaps the best one of all. If you are going to write one, refer to Chapter 13. Enough cannot be said about self-publishing, you being the publisher, if you are going to write a book as part of your program. It is a critical element to generating income if you decide to write a book.

> *It takes one hour of preparation*
> *for each minute of presentation time.*
> —WAYNE BURGRAFF, 18TH CENTURY AMERICAN PHILOSOPHER

CHAPTER 18

INTERNET MARKETING

Your website has been designed, your products have been packaged, your merchant account to process credit cards has been established, your autoresponder is installed, now you are waiting for customers to come to your site.

Your website or page designer has submitted keywords for your website to the search engines. There are literally thousands of search engines out there but some of the big ones are Google®, AllTheWeb®, AltaVista® and Northern Lights®.

When a search engine finds your website and then places it at some point in its index, you have become ranked.

Being new you will probably be lost in the crowd on the big search engines. You may fare better on the smaller ones but obviously you cannot rely on those placements alone to drive traffic to your site. If you do, it will be a long wait so you must take action to let the folks in cyberworld know you are open for business.

There are two ways to do this. The first requires some advertising money and consists of four popular methods: joint ventures, banners, pay-per-click and paid e-zine ads. The second does not require money and is free. We will explore the free method first.

Free E-zine articles—The best free method. In the world of cyberspace there are publications called e-zines—electronic magazines. There are thousands of them, perhaps tens of thousands. The publishers of these e-zines are always looking for pertinent material to fill up space in their publications. These publications build up mailing lists called double opt-in lists which means the subscriber confirms his registration to insure against spamming, which is illegal.

They will happily feature anything you write that is pertinent to their readers' interest considering, of course, that it conforms to the basic standards of punctuation and grammar. We are not talking about great literature here but, instructive, non-fiction fare. Big interest areas are self-help, how-to, financial and lifestyle material. When your article is published, there will be a connecting link to the home page (main page) of your website. Any reader who finds your article to be of interest can zip right off to your website to get to know you and perhaps buy from you.

How do you find the e-zines that will publish your work? Interestingly enough, they will find you. Here's how it works. There are directories to whom you submit your material such as the Directory of Ezines at *www.directoryofezines.com* and Go-

Ezines at *www.go-ezines.com*. There are many more and you can find them if you go to *www.Google.com* and punch in e-zines.

When you do, you will also see opportunities for starting your own e-zine which you may consider doing at a later date but to start up, focus on the articles. This can be very effective because you will be attracting your target audience and you can build it successfully that way. It is the best way to attract buying traffic.

If you can write a simple sentence, string several together into an article about your area of interest. It will be worth it.

Free Ads—As mentioned there are, in existence, thousands of e-zines. In order to attract more subscribers so the publisher can build his or her list in order to lure paying advertisers, they will offer free ads to lure you. This the publisher will do either individually or banding together with other publishers to build the big subscriber number to get your attention. This is a shotgun method where your ad is being sent to hordes of people, many with no interest in your product or service. Take advantage of it. You might get something. It is free, but remember, you usually get what you pay for.

Free Blogs—You can drive traffic to your sales website with a blog. What is a blog? Think newspaper column and you are close except that a blog is interactive. Your readers can get right back to you. As a business tool you can attract new visitors to your blog then redirect them to your business site with a link and a promise of a special offer.

The key to this is the content of the blog. It must be related to what you sell to make it work and it must have a slant that attracts people. If it does, you can develop a following and that generates buzz which will create even more viewers.

One more thing: If you use strategic keywords and certain links to specific websites, your search engine ratings can start to climb… for both the blog and the business site.

Joint Venture—It will cost you but the money is not up front and you will usually get results. The Internet has spawned a unique trading process called the joint venture where two or more websites join together in a promotion or special sale. It can be a venture by equal partners or it can be a senior-junior kind of arrangement where the senior would be the originator of the venture to promote his product. The junior would simply endorse the senior's product with a testimonial to the people on his or her list. The net result of a joint venture would be sales, of course, recognition because you would be creating an impact, and if it is newsworthy, the making of a good press release. Lastly, the sales coming from outside your own list would be added to your list. And that is very important since they will go into your database for future contact.

Banners—An effective advertising medium on the Internet, the banner ad is a small ad of various configuration that you can place, for a fee, on a website with heavy traffic. The viewers on that site, when seeing your little ad, can click on it and be immediately transported to your website. That is called a click-through and its full effectiveness is realized when the person buys your product.

A secondary benefit is the branding, the impact the image has on the mind of the viewer that may activate him to buy your product at a later time. The term "page view "or " impression" is the means of gauging the number of times viewers have seen the page your ad is on. Banner ads are usually sold on that basis, i.e., cost per thousand impressions.

A typical medium on which you might advertise with banners is Arcamax Publishing® at *www.Arcamax.com*. This is as close to a newspaper type of website that you will find on the web and it reaches 1.5 million subscribers. Because of its makeup, you can target your audience. There are many other sites you could consider for ad placement. One way to gauge a site you are considering is to check it out on *www.Alexa.com*. This website will give you a reality check on just what websites offer in the way of audience numbers.

Pay per click—This is an advertising technique of the search engines that provides you with banner ad placement and your payment is based on the response of the viewer. You pay per click.

It has some interesting aspects, one of them being that you bid for a price per click against others with interests similar to yours. You vie for the placement of your ad on sites that typically draw viewers interested in your type of product. Those ads are placed on key websites that would attract people you are trying to reach and the ads appear as banners.

Yahoo provides a means for testing the effectiveness of key-words by checking the drawing power of key words. If you go to *http://inventory.overture.com* and punch in a keyword or term, you will see the number of times in the past month that partic-ular word or term was sought. If I clicked in *career change* in March, 2006 we would see that 356,967 came up in the previous February.

The bidding is for the keywords applicable to the nature or description of your site. Sites with a similar theme might vie for the same keyword, i.e., a site dealing with the Civil War might opt for the term Civil War. Since everyone in that genre would want that keyword, the bidding could rise beyond cost-effectiveness for many. Those not wishing to go top dollar might find it effec-tive to use keywords like Gettysburg, Civil War battles or Civil War campaigns which could be secured for lower bids, yet they would obviously attract viewers interested in the Civil War.

It is a matter of perception. Keep in mind that you are basi-cally allocating funds dedicated to those keywords. The more funds you put into it, the more your ad can appear per month all over the net. Do not let the word "bid" distract you. You can budget as little as $50 a month for this service.

Google, the thousand pound gorilla on the Internet, has a serv-ice called Adword which we just touched on. Yahoo® has a similar service which used to be called Overture, but now functions under the name Yahoo! Search Marketing®. Check out the fine print on these and all the other search engine programs. It can be an important avenue for you.

E-zine ads—This is a very economical way of advertising. E-zines, as a rule, do not charge much for ads. The ads usually appear at the head of the e-zine much the way of a classified ad. The value of this type of advertising is that it is not only a cost-effective way to go but you can target your ads. There are e-zines for every subject and the directories (go to Google or Yahoo) will help you find them and will spell out the subscription numbers. Starting up, you should definitely consider factoring in this type of advertising. I have seen targeted ads to 100,000 subscribers for as little as $10.

When starting out you will find yourself under siege. Your URL will be public information and easily accessible. The bombardment will be offers of all sort, many assuring you that they have the answers that will assure you of big bucks at the end of the month. Beware. It is easy to lose focus. Do not stray from your business plan. If some offers seem to be the real thing, that can add to your plan. Do your homework first. Approach with caution.

Many a small thing has been made large
by the right kind of advertising.
—MARK TWAIN

Other Internet Opportunities

Recruiting Affiliates

Sometimes called associates, traffic can be built up by recruiting affiliates which are websites that function as traffic generators for your site.

It is the placement of a link, like a banner ad, on the affiliate website for your product. When it is clicked, the clicker is transported to your site like the banner ad. It is a commission arrangement.

Recompense can be in a variety of ways. It can be based on the number of people the affiliate sends to your site, which is called pay-per-click, or the number of people who buy something, which is called pay-per-sale.

It could also be based on some other factor such as registering on your site for your opt-in list or the number of people visiting your site. This would be called pay-per-lead. Everything is negotiable and just about everybody is approachable.

Oh yes, one other important thing: Recruiting affiliates has another benefit, too. Exposure. You are getting advertising. Your name is being seen by the flow of humanity on the byways and highways out there in cyberspace.

Being an Affiliate. Income can be generated by doing the reverse of above. You can become an affiliate. Amazon, Barnes and Noble and a veritable host of companies would love to engage you as an affiliate. When you are set-up and have a sense of the type of firms that would be compatible with yours, start looking around.

Amazon started the affiliate concept using the designation of Associate. Check Amazon out by going to *www.Amazon.com* and pressing the Associate tab on the bottom of the page. You will find the specifics there. Then for a broader look at sources, go to a directory such as Affiliate Programs at *www.affiliatematch.com* and you will get a listing by subject. You will find more such in directories on the search engines.

More Marketing

The channels through which you can market your products would not have been recognizable ten years ago. Change, of course, has brought them to be. They are the seminar, tele-seminar and *Amazon.com*. I include the seminar as a change because it is a booming business because of the Internet. Let's look at that first.

Seminars

If the word seminar evokes thoughts of speaking in public and awakens the rumblings of panic in your visceral depths, hold on, don't panic. Let's talk seminar first then we'll deal with your anxiety.

The seminar today is a booming business. People across the land are doing it and making a living at it. Companies, too, have formed to provide seminars on a wide variety of subjects and are thriving.

Gwen Moran, writing in *Entrepreneur Magazine*, said much the same.

"Anyone who's attended an interesting and informative seminar knows it can be one of the best ways to train staff, keep yourself up-to-date on industry changes and learn new skills. On the flip side, seminars are also a powerful way to build awareness of your company, market your products or services, and possibly create a new revenue stream for your business. Whatever type of business you're in, you probably have knowledge and expertise that others would find helpful—and that might encourage them to use your services."

There are seminars on just about any topic. Think of a subject, you'll find a seminar. Just go to the website *www.finda seminar.com* and you will see more than a few.

I used to run what amounted to a seminar every Monday on salesmanship for three years and I have sat in on some either to learn something or to examine the structure of the event. Seminars can range from a cerebral flow of information you might find in the insurance or financial field to a co-operatively sponsored event of self-help suppliers offering information laced with waves of hope, inspiration and enthusiasm.

Often situated in a moderately priced hotel like the Holiday Inn or Best Western, seminars are charging about $150 and up, per person for an all-day event.

Companies like SkillPath Seminars® that specializes in seminars advertised for a Corpus Christi, Texas seminar on debt collection for $179 and in Grand Forks, North Dakota their fee was listed at $199 for a seminar on controlling priorities.

And in New York a couple of self-help suppliers in enlightenment are getting $20 per person in a school room setting for 180 minutes on instantaneous transformation. For a full weekend, the same couple are hosting an event for $400 a head at a theater club with the subject being access to enlightenment.

There are seminars across the land on subjects ranging from writing plays to gambling and from belly dancing to letting loose the inner goddess. And there are even seminars on how to do... you guessed it... *seminars.*

Yes, Fred Gleeck does just that and he has also written *Marketing and Promoting your own Seminars and Workshops* which is a very good blueprint for doing seminars.

An effective technique when you are starting out doing seminars is to have a joint venture. This is when there is participation by one or more companies to host the seminar. This works well in the hotel seminar where the costs are shared and, very importantly, a dynamic is created that generates enthusiasm and enthusiasm can always result in sales.

Once you have stepped into the water, it will be important to network with others who have complementary interests to yours. This can easily be done through the Internet. There is definitely power in numbers.

Now let's talk for a moment about that fear you have of public speaking. Everyone seems to have some of it. Studies show that it is the primary fear in most of us, more so than walking down an unfamiliar alley on a dark night.

I used to have a lot of it and by virtue of all the speaking I have done over the years it has lessened considerably but there is still something that springs up "down there" that goes to work when I approach the podium. Friends who speak publically tell me the same thing and they all agree it is a good thing. It makes them prepare.

If you would like to do it, you can. There are books on the subject that will help you. You will find some in the resource section of this book, however, my strongest recommendation is Toastmasters International based on several friends who went through it. The difference I saw in them was remarkable. Membership fee is very reasonable, it offers a hands-on approach coupled with a social aspect and there are chapters all over the country. If the fear of speaking has a strong grip on your innards, check out Toastmasters. Even though the thought may be paralyzing, check it out. It won't hurt you.

Tele-seminars

One of the best kept secrets in the world of marketing is the low cost of tele-seminars. Because it is so cost-effective, it is one of the aspects of the seminar world that is starting to surge. It is the conducting of a seminar on the telephone. This is where your advertising directs a lot of people to dial in to your seminar.

There are two forms to this method: the fee-charged seminar where you enroll people for a fee to benefit from your knowledge and the free seminar which you use to interest people in buying your information at a follow-up time.

Your campaign to get people to enroll in the free or fee-based seminar can be based on a number of techniques. The most commonly used one today appears to be the joint-venture which we looked at earlier. This is when a percentage of the enrollment fee is paid out to websites with some similarity to your own who interest their following in your service and enroll them for you or direct them to you. They get a commission for their successful efforts.

Advertising in Internet magazines—ezines—is another way we looked at earlier. They are very inexpensive as we noted. Setting up a tele-seminar is very easy and, as mentioned, relatively inexpensive. Companies that provide this service charge either a "by the minute" fee of about five cents a minute per line or a flat fee per line. The latter is the way to go.

This can be done through such services as Brainwave Communications®, a San Diego based firm, that offers a flat rate on a very reasonable monthly basis with unlimited usage 24/7.

The rate is set on the number of lines you require. Brainwave's rates, at this writing, are $59.95 for ten lines and $295 for 100. Rates for higher—up to 5000 actually—and in between numbers are available but you get the idea. You can connect with them at *www.bwc.com*.

Amazon.com

Amazon is a miracle. It started out selling books a little over 10 years ago and today it is the largest department store on the Internet doing a reported sales volume of $8.49 billion in 2005.

Amazon has those numbers because it sells everything from a $5 book to a $39,000 fur coat. Amazon has 32 categories of product that it sells to the world at large. Somewhere in those 32 categories that finds exposure in all 50 states and a host of countries, you may well be able to place your product so it may be part of Amazon's remarkable phenomena.

How do you do that?

If the information product you come up with is a book, video, music or DVD and you have North American distribution rights (which you undoubtedly will have) and your product meets normal publishing standards or an audio that meets Amazon's standards—which are not difficult to meet—you'll be in business. To find out what those standards are go to *www.Amazon.com* and check in at the Advantage Program. You will get all the information there.

Jude Wright of Chino Hills, California, is a successful entrepreneur on the Internet. She designs websites and writes and publishes e-zines, and is also an affiliate. When she started out on the Internet, she had learned an important lesson. Here is her story as she tells it:

"For 25 years of my life, my jobs progressed from clerk to secretary to administrative assistant, bookkeeper and office manager. I worked most of those years in the construction industry and the last four in manufacturing and warehousing.

I never thought that I would do anything else. I figured that I would simply retire, take care of my house, and maybe do some traveling. Circumstances dictated a different path.

My husband and I purchased one of those "get rich quick" programs that we saw on television. Well, that scam cost us several thousand dollars, but it did get me interested. I was hooked by the possibilities that I saw and I knew that money could be made if I went about it the right way.

I continued to work at my "day job" for the next two years while studying everything I could find on Internet marketing. When I retired from work to care for my elderly father-in-law, I had more time to work on my business, and I started to make a profit. The money that was lost by investing in that scam has now been regained.

I started creating my own websites and realized that I was more interested in designing websites than I was in promoting them. Now, about half of my income comes from designing websites and the graphics that are used on the Internet.

Even though I have to work harder than I did at many of my clerical positions, I am enjoying the work much more. I am free to take short vacations to visit my children and grandchildren. And I can work from any place that has an Internet connection. For me, it is ideal.

I publish two e-zines or online newsletters. The e-zines keep me in contact with my website visitors and they provide my readers with information about my websites. I also introduce them to products that I believe will help them in their online business.

I started my *www.nutritious-cooking.com* site because of my interest in healthy recipes. Little did I know that this would become one of my most popular websites. The website generates income from affiliate products. I receive a commission when someone purchases a product from a recommendation I have given for it.

I make money with the e-zines from two sources. The first is from advertising. People pay me to advertise in my newsletters. I also get income from affiliate products that I show to my readers." Jude Wright is the owner of numerous websites. You can reach her at *http://wrightwayservices.com*. Her e-mail address is *jude@judewright.com*.

Private information is practically the source of every large modern fortune.

—OSCAR WILDE

Thoughts

1. Before writing your ad, know for whom you are writing. Know how she thinks and what she wants.
2. When you know the person for whom you are writing, fashion an ad that will fit her like a tailored suit.
3. Your customer often reads advertisements in order to find something that will improve her life, even though she doesn't quite know what that thing is.

4. When writing the ad, remember that the headline is the most important part of it. It is the part that interests the reader or viewer to search the body of the ad. And what is he searching for? The benefit to him. Something that will make his life better in some way.

5. It is important to remember that the reader of your ad may not be consciously aware of your product, much less know he has a need for it. Your ad should awaken that need and drive him to take the action of ordering it.

ORGANIZING THINGS

The Business Plan

Before you start out, it is critically important that you know where you are heading or where you want to go. If you don't have an idea and a detailed plan, your likelihood of success is not very likely at all.

The business plan can come in many forms. Some are designed to pursue capital and loans from investors and banks and can take up to a hundred pages or more.

You need not burden yourself with such a document since the ventures with which we are dealing do not require heavy or even moderate capital so do not let the notion of writing a business plan deter you. Let's get to it.

A simple business plan defines your business, your goals and objectives, and is your tracking sheet. Prior to doing that you must have concluded the two preliminaries.

Preliminary one. Looked for change. Checked your market to see if it is emerging.

Preliminary two. Checked to see if the market was viable, had a rich core target.

If the two preliminaries are positive, here are some suggested steps:

Step One. In order to crystallize your business, describe it on paper.

1. Describe your business. Write everything about it that comes to mind.
2. The steps you will take to put it together.
3. The steps you will take to market your information. Start off with a description of the image you wish to project. Be succinct. One sentence.
4. Determine how you will project that image.
5. The goals you expect to reach and when you will reach them. Be sure to include the intermediate time goals. This will help you to keep a grasp on things.

Step Two. You are in business to make a profit and develop an income stream. You will be providing some capital, no matter how small, to start your business. You have to track it to see it turn into that profit.

1. Become familiar with the basic accounting forms: cash flow analysis, profit and loss statement and balance sheet. Implement them at the appropriate time.
2. Set up a cash flow analysis to keep a firm grasp on your growth.

3. Check with an accountant about tax liability.

4. Draw up a Profit and Loss Statement and establish a Balance Sheet. This will be done quarterly and will give you a clear picture of your assets, liabilities and the worth of your business. You can get free templates of all the accounting forms at the Small Business Administration's site at *http://www.sba.gov/library/forms.html#financial.*

5. When business starts to happen, it is important to keep a tight control on it. It would be wise to get an accountant when the numbers start to mount. The value of an accountant lies not in his sage advice at tax time but in his sage advice long before tax time when he can advise you on things to do so when tax time arrives the pain is minimal.

Marketing 101

Critical to your business plan is the marketing component. You must lay out the route you will take to meet your goals. This is no different, in a sense, than setting out on an automobile trip from Des Moines, Iowa to Purdy's Corner in upstate New York without a road map.

You must know where you want to go and you must mark out the route you will take. It is called marketing.

What is Marketing?

It is what your business is all about. It is why you opened shop. Marketing has two primary components that you should never forget.

1. The customer's needs are primary. They need to be satisfied. That is your purpose.
2. You must satisfy those needs for a profit.

How do you realize those needs?

Through market research

Spotting of trends, population shifts, economic shifts.

Selection of target market

A determination of a group that will respond to your offering.

Through advantage analysis

Focusing on the target market and determining the edge you will have over others in the market.

Media research

This should be called website research because you must see what is on the web. You will get ideas for putting a website together, what you can do and how to do it. You will need this information if you design a site yourself or to pass on to a web master if you elect to hire one.

If you have limited capital, this process enables you to concentrate your efforts on a key segment of the market as we saw with the New-Irish food hypothetical case.

There we focused on a segment of the market. You should do the same.

Once past the research phase and into the structural phase, four aspects come into play.

Your information product

This is where your creative juices can flow and you can have fun doing it, too. After you have decided what the nature of your information is, make a CD outlining it, interview someone you can promote as being important or accomplished in your field, form a club in your specialty and give benefits for a reasonable membership fee.

The pricing, distribution and promotion

You are dealing with information. It has a different value to different people. Do not come in too low. That may be a tendency but it will be a mistake if you do. Come in on the high side. The quality of your work will be perceived as having greater value.

The distribution is direct and the promotion should be in joint ventures and e-zine articles.

All aspects mentioned above should be spelled out on paper. Everything.

And it doesn't stop there.

If you were in that automobile traveling from Des Moines to Purdy's Corner, you would be pulling out that road map periodically. So too with the business plan.

A periodic look-see is mandatory if you are to stay on target. Be sure to do it.

If you would like guidance on writing a formal business plan, the Small Business Administration has put together an excellent tutorial that you can see at *http://www.sba.gov/starting_business/planning/basic.html.* It is informative and takes you through the process with the help of animations and audio description. You would do well to check it out.

Forms

Business forms are an integral part of doing business. There are more business forms than any one person will ever need and they are all available, at no charge, at the Small Business Administration's website. You can download them at *http://www.sba.gov/library/forms.html.*

T h o u g h t s

1. In the world of the Internet, it is useless to be creative unless you can also sell what you create. Your prospect cannot recognize a good idea unless it is presented to them by an effective sales piece.

2. When you sell on the Internet, stay focused so your prospect's mind takes in what you tell them. You must lead them to take the action of making a purchase. Every unnecessary word is a distraction that only serves to weaken the call to action.

3. The seminar can be a vital adjunct to your marketing effort. The seminar itself is often an adjunct to "back-of-the-room" sales in that it gives you a dual income stream.

4. The telephone seminar is a unique way of getting tens, hundreds and even thousands of people together without leaving your office. It is the most cost effective means of marketing today for the small business person.

5. *Amazon.com* is literally a window on the world. It is very possible your product on Amazon can be sold in countries in virtually every continent in the world.

Do you know what amazes me more than anything else? The impotence of force to organize anything.

—NAPOLEON BONAPARTE

CHAPTER

GETTING ENDORSEMENTS

E ndorsements are very helpful because they are a form of proof that what you say is true. They are also one of the most important elements in the sales letter.

When someone is reading your sales letter, book cover or promotion piece, favorable comments by a well-known, or at least a known personality blended into the sales material helps to close the sale. It is, in the mind of the reader, a certification that the product you are selling is all that your sales or promotion piece says it is. And psychologically it is more. You will find out why in a following chapter.

As you know, you are constantly subjected to the blandishments of salesmen, sales letters and what the courts call sales puffery. You have a built-in sales resistance.

Everyone has it.

Testimonials help you get past that resistance. The testimonial subtly says to the reader: You can believe this. I guarantee it.

So how can you get famous people you don't know to guarantee what you say is true?

First, your program, product, book or whatever it is you are selling has to be good and worthwhile. That being said the rest is a simple process of numbers and reaching out and by that, I mean getting to know your target folk who will say something nice about your product.

Before you do that, however, please bear in mind that celebrities have feelings like you. The *persona* you see is rarely the real person.

They have all the feelings you looked at earlier in the book. They laugh, cry, grieve, rejoice, celebrate and all the rest. They are very human.

When I was in college in New York City in the '50s, I was fortunate to have a great weekend job for four years working backstage for the Jackie Gleason and Ed Sullivan shows. I got to see first hand the makeup of hundreds if not thousands of celebrities and among the many things I noticed about them as a group of people is their need for approval. Their work is constantly in the public view so they are always subject to public criticism and very open to words of approval.

When you approach one, your request for a blurb or testimonial is an obvious form of approval. It is an ego stroke, it is praise.

It is also publicity. And that's something else I noticed about them during my four years at CBS Television. They like publicity. It is an integral part of their business. Their careers thrive on it. It is a tool of their trade.

But they still don't know you, so when you approach them, approach them softly.

If it is for a book you can make a fairly direct approach because books have a cachet that commands interest.

Dan Poynter, in his book, *The Self-Publishing Manual*, suggests contacting celebrities with a suggested blurb and copies of the table of contents, a chapter of the book and a mock-up of the cover along with a cover letter. If you are writing a book, you should read Poynter's *Self-Publishing Manual*. It includes a sample cover letter.

Celebrity addresses can be obtained in publications such as *The Ultimate Celebrity Black Book* and at websites such as *Contact Any Celebrity* at *www.contactanycelebrity.com*.

There appears to be an affiliation between the two. The website has 54,000 names and addresses and you can subscribe for $19 a month with a one month minimum. The book is $55 for the 54,000 names.

If you have a project other than a book, you might want to consider a softer approach. Compile a list of names that would be a fit for your project. Then go to a website like The Quotations Page at *http://www.quotationspage.com/* or Cybernation at *www.cybernation.com* and check out the quotations made by your list members, then write to them and ask for permission to use their quotes for your project.

Even though their quotations are a listed matter, you should still get their approval to use them. It is a courtesy and it is an ice breaker.

And it is publicity for them.

For each ten you send out, you should receive about four positive replies. High profile people tend to be on the move and the other six may not have caught up, were lost or ignored by a third party.

Upon receipt of those responses, write a simple handwritten note of thanks on nice stationary. This will make a favorable impression because such proprieties have become a rarity.

Then two weeks later write the request for the blurb and make it easy for them. Write a cover letter explaining the worthwhile purpose and on a second sheet write a suggested blurb, leaving room for a more preferable blurb if desired and a space for the signature.

All the celebrity has to do is agree with a checkmark or pen in his or her own blurb and put it in the accompanying stamped, self-addressed envelope which you will have included.

It is advisable to use priority mail both to the individual and for the return reply. It not only expedites matters but it underscores importance.

Note: In the celebrity contact book or website, the office of the celebrity's agent is often listed as the address. I suggest you call and touch base with the agent who is usually very positive on the subject and will be looking for it. You should follow up with the agent to confirm receipt of your request after a proper interval.

*Without question, when people are uncertain,
they are more likely to use others' actions to
decide how they themselves should act.*

—ROBERT CIALDINI, PH.D.,

INFLUENCE: THE PSYCHOLOGY OF PERSUASION

CHAPTER

THE FORMULA
FOR SUCCESS

The key to any success is planning and an integral part of that planning is a guide. When Sir Edmund Hillary climbed Mount Everest, it was his Sherpa companion Tensing Gorgay who guided him to the top.

Your guide up your personal mountain will be a formula which will take you up the winding path to the top.

It will be the structure for your golden opportunity.

The formula for success is:

$$R = B + F + P + A$$

B is belief in yourself. Without this you can't do anything. Author and motivator Claude Bristol wrote that every person is the creation of him and her self, the image of his or her own thinking and believing. As individuals think and believe, so they are.

You are what you think you are. Always remember that. You are a composite of many things. Your successes and disappointments are entwined with the readings and influences of your life with special emphasis on the influences of your family, friends and teachers in early life. It is a vital requirement that you think well of yourself in order to achieve success. The first and most important step toward success is the feeling that you can succeed.

> *Confidence is contagious and so is lack of confidence,*
> *and a customer will recognize both.*
> —VINCE LOMBARDI

F is focus. You have to keep your eye on what you are doing and the goal you have established. This is where self-discipline and life management come in. The former, of course, is doing from habit or routine what one must do; the latter is channeling your efforts into one strong river of effort. It is diverting your various streams of activity into one powerful force of energy which will sweep you past obstacles that previously blocked your way. Keep your eye on the immediate change you wish to make and results will follow. Do this a change at a time and you will reach your goal. This is staying focused.

> *The shortest way to do many things*
> *is to do only one thing at a time.*
> —SYDNEY SMILES, 18TH CENTURY ESSAYIST

P is for preparation or planning. Putting the information you have acquired over the years into package form, setting up the little things that make for a small business (there are no big things) and preparing a plan (not very complicated but absolutely necessary). This is setting up shop. Designing your inventory (your information and the format in which you will make it available), filling out and filing the paperwork that makes you a business and outlining the steps you will take to reach your goal. This is where the entrepreneur in you comes out, your creativity, decisiveness and energy.

The essential ingredient in constructing anything—be it an airplane, a Saturn rocket or a small business—is a plan from which to build the object. Without it the airplane, the rocket and the business will never get off the ground.

> *Always plan. It wasn't raining when*
> *Noah built the ark.*
> —RICHARD M. CUSHING, CLERGYMAN

A is for action. Taking it to market. This is the fun part. Some call it marketing, others selling. Call it what you will, to render your information, in whatever form it may be for coin of the realm, is the true exercise of your career of gold.

> *Everyone lives by selling something.*
> —ROBERT LOUIS STEVENSON

R is for results. If you follow your plan R could also be S for success. And in this you will find a gratification like no other.

> *Some of us will do our jobs well and some*
> *will not, but we will all be judged*
> *by only one thing—the result.*
> —Vince Lombardi

Thoughts

1. A formula is just a guide. The person who uses it gives it meaning. It is impossible to climb a mountain while sitting in a chair so get on your feet, use the formula and start off.

2. You can make your luck. Prepare. When you climb the heights, never give up. You will get the hang of the climb quickly enough.

3. Be aware that reality contains great beauty. You can discover much of it as you pursue your career of gold. Prepare for the ever-changing scenery as you climb and when you reach the heights your view will be unobstructed.

4. When you are motivated by your passion to reach the top you are entering that special place in life that has deep meaning. Know your passion and use it.

22
CHAPTER

MORE
MARKETING 101

It is easy to develop lists to follow and say this is how you do it. If you have actually done it you cannot let it go at that. There is much more to it than a mere list. It is the day-to-day search for opportunity which in time turns into an automatic search programmed by the subconscious.

You are doing it and you don't even realize you are doing it. That's one of the hallmarks of being an entrepreneur.

But let's go to the list first, then we'll touch on the day-to-day reality.

Selling is the soul of business. It keeps everybody else employed. Let's look at the key factors for selling. Whether you are speaking on an audio, showing up on a video or writing a sales letter (which most of you will probably do), the following applies equally.

In the section on writing sales letters, I mentioned the up front admission of the products limitations. In this list it is again item number one following the attention getter.

Get attention. State a reason your information package is being made available. Your headline, so to speak.

1. In the first sentence it should be stated or implied that the product is not perfect, that God or nature may have come up with something a little better and that man (you) in his imperfection was unable to do any better. But this is still pretty good. Specify or imply what it doesn't do.

2. Spell out the benefits. You have credibility at this point. Tell your benefits. Don't exaggerate. This is what your client or customer will buy from you, not the CD or the e-book or even a real book. They will buy from you what *the information contained* in those items will do for them.

When dealing with specialized markets like environmentalists, horses, dogs, food and the like, you have a fairly direct line on what the benefits might be for those in your target audience. Additionally to those and all other markets there are crossover benefits that those in the target market have as humans.

Those ten key selling benefits are:

*   Making money
    We can never get enough of it. It is the answer to a lot of problems and prayers.

- Saving money

  (Note: This should be presented as avoiding the *loss* of money.) People will go to great lengths to avoid a loss, far greater than *saving* money. The word *loss* has much greater impact.

- Lessen pain

  This is something the human being responds to because pain impacts on life in several negative ways. It is natural to seek relief from it.

  Those people afflicted with an ailment that your information can alleviate will tune in automatically.

- Ego enrichment

  This is manifested in several ways ranging from physical beauty to status. Everyone has some of it.

- Make life easier

  Creatures of comfort (Homo sapiens) are always seeking new ways to increase their comfort. It is part of the culture. Note that in this, there may be a tie-in with ego enrichment. Bigger this, bigger that, more than the neighbor's, faster than the neighbor's, etc.

- Avoid loss

  Loss is to be avoided. It is part of the cultures of indulgence, possession and centeredness. To lose something is to be lessened.

- Physical safety
  Survival is Homo sapiens greatest natural instinct.
- To save time
  Time is a precious commodity because the pressures of modern life are very stressful. Stress relief can equate with physical relief.
- Sexual attraction
  The second greatest instinct in Homo sapiens is sex. Attracting the opposite sex is a very basic need for one to have a feeling of well-being. The rest on this subject is obvious.
- Look younger
  Several factors here. Ego, enamored with self, acceptance to youth culture, avoidance of aging, sexual attraction.

Selling is a simple matter of thinking of the other person and what he or she will get from your product. Do not think of yourself because your customer does not. The one thing that matters is that your customer's needs are being satisfied: That is your customer's sole concern. Please remember the world works on self-interest. Everyone acts to enhance his position. Everyone. Even you. When you are preparing your sales material think of your customer and his self-interest. Satisfy that and you will have a sale.

CHAPTER

THE BEST KEPT SECRET IN MARKETING

There is a subject that most writers do not touch on for whatever reason. Perhaps it is because the information could be used the wrong way as it has been throughout the ages. Some have realized the truth of it, acted on it for their own benefit, often to the detriment of others.

Today that secret is used by some in the corporate world for the purpose of manipulation, so too by some people pursuing power in the world of politics.

Not all to be sure, but some.

I will share this with you since you are most likely at an age where your sense of judgement is good and your use of this information would be used in a positive way.

I will preface what I am about to say with a little self-assessment. I have organizational skills, I am trusting and early in my life I had political ambitions. OK. Enough said on that.

Forty years ago from this writing when I was a youth of 30, I coordinated a few political campaigns for office holders and seekers in one of the major parties. It was county and congressional stuff.

One of the earliest things I studied were voting patterns. I learned that in any given area you could count on a certain number of votes. No matter what kind of candidate you put up, Attila the Hun reincarnated, he could get that number of votes.

While doing the campaign for re-election of a congressman, I sought to get him the nomination of a third party. Since my childhood, this particular third party had been a fixture in my state, was well-known and had a cachet that attracted individuals who projected an image of the thinking intellectual.

Two individuals seemed to head the third party so I made an appointment to meet with them to discuss the nomination. Perhaps, if we got that, we might get some financial support as well. This was before primaries were used to select candidates.

They were open to the possibility, I was told. They would give serious consideration to it.

"What about your convention to select? When will that be held?" I enquired.

They hemmed and hawed. There would be no convention.

"Well, how do your committemen select a candidate?"

There were no committemen or committeewomen.

The fact was there was no money either.

There was no functioning party. Just an image, an illusion.

The meeting for their purpose was to get some financing *from us*, to be perceived as players, to be able to stay on the ballot and to get exposure in the press. And if we were successful, some political leverage.

I had some difficulty adjusting to this new reality because my perception since childhood was that the party was a *bona fide* force in the state.

As reality set in, *we* agreed to finance a big rally for our candidate under *their* banner. It was summertime. We would make it a big outdoor affair for *their* people and they would send out word to their people.

As the affair began, no one had come. The words sent out to their people had apparently not arrived. The party was fast becoming a non-event.

We hurriedly gathered our committee people, campaign volunteers and any one else who wanted free beer, pizza and hot dogs to assemble for a few pictures. The press was fortunately late, took a few pictures when they arrived and left. We were not totally embarrassed.

The story here is that the third party that attracted the intellectual thinker was hollow. There was nothing there but a cachet that attracted those voters to cast their ballot for our candidate on their ticket rather than our ticket which was more representative of the candidate's beliefs. When the intellectual thinkers voted that party, they were casting their vote for an allusion, a man who didn't share all the beliefs they typically held.

I came to realize that if Donald Duck had been nominated and dressed in a beret and a rumpled sweater, he would have gotten the same number of votes.

People will respond to allusion, we've all fallen victim to it, but that is not the secret.

The marketing secret is that people will fall for illusion and other techniques of deception because *they don't think.* Very few people do because it is easier to get by without thinking. It is much easier to follow along than to step out and lead.

Clearly the "intellectual thinkers" were not thinking when they cast their votes 40 years ago.

They were acting, as we all do from time to time, in a manner learned from childhood, a manner based on learning rather than thinking.

Psychologist Robert Cialdini in his book, *Influence: The Power of Persuasion,* maintains that only five percent of people think. This might appear to contrast with Pareto Law which maintains the 80–20 principle that we looked at earlier. But it may not.

It is my experience that the 20 percent individuals do so for a variety of reasons. Some produce moderately or at least fairly well on a consistent basis. They are regimented and do the same thing that works for them consistently. It is the few though, who consistently lead the pack in production. They have figured out a way or ways to top the charts. They are the true thinkers. Perhaps Cialdini's five percent holds up. At least it is approximate.

Thinking is not learning. They are two different processes. Because we humans learn very well, we are the primary species on the planet.

But what we do with what we learn is something else. And now we are getting to the nub of the secret.

According to *New Scientist Magazine,* April 1, 2006, a study indicates that we humans learn by imitating at an early age. We humans have a massive amount to learn and children need to learn quickly. Imitating parents and others accomplishes that. It provides the child with a ready-made solution to the learning problem.

And it doesn't end with childhood. It carries on.

Think for a moment about your own life. You are probably what you are because your parents started you doing what they did. Your religion, your politics, your cultural tastes to name a few things. You have accepted from authorities.

And there you have it. The acceptance from authorities you know.

We act on that acceptance, accept it as true, and rarely do we question it. It's in our subconscious.

Now start thinking. How has that been used in politics, say in Germany? How is it used in business, in advertisements in the U. S.? How is it being used in nation building in Iraq?

Now how will you use it?

The power of thought, the magic of the mind.

—LORD BYRON

CHAPTER

A LAST WORD

We are living in uncertain times. Social Security, pensions and health insurance, factors that were established to lend comfort to our lives, are threatened by the ever weakening dollar and the strangling grip of price escalation.

A malaise seems to have gripped the political process as well, for little has been done to alleviate those problems. As the problems mount, the capacity for understanding and resolving their magnitude can only diminish.

Those of us who prepared for the senior years with funding accumulated during earlier years are discovering that we may live long past our financial ability to sustain ourselves.

Some have no concern about such matters while others are very concerned and are disposed to hope and wait for the government to resolve those matters.

And there are others who are concerned and are willing to do something about it and are stepping forth or are willing to step forth, to do just that. For those, I hope this book will be of help in some small way.

RESOURCES

EMOTIONAL INTELLIGENCE

Bibliography/Recommended Reading

Books

Goleman, Daniel (1995) *Emotional Intelligence: Why it can matter more than IQ* New York: Bantam

Bloomfield, Harold (2001) *Making Peace With Your Past: The Six Essential Steps to Enjoying a Great Future* New York: Harper

Weisinger, Hendrie (2000) *Emotional Intelligence at Work* Jossey-Bass: New Ed edition

Bradberry T. and Jean Greave (2000) *The Emotional Intelligence Quickbook: Everything You Need to Know to put your Emotional Intelligence to Work* Jossey-Bass

Websites

www.haygroup.com

www.funderstanding.com/eq.cfm-9k

www.6seconds.org

www.missionpossibleinc.com/case.htm

Websites for Testing your EQ

www.haygroup.com/resources/default_ieitest.htm

www.helpself.com/iq-test.htm-16k

www.6seconds.org

www.myskillsprofile.com/

CREATIVITY

Bibliography/Recommended Reading

Ward, Thomas B., Ronald Finke and Steven Smith 1995 *Creativity and the Mind: Discovering the Genius Within* Plenum Press

Carter, Ronald (2004) *Language and Creativity: The Art of Common Talk* Routledge

Miller, William C. (1999) *Flash of Brilliance: Inspiring Creativity Where You Work* Perseus Books (Current Publisher: Perseus Publishing)

Cameron, Julia (1996) *The Vein of Gold. A journey to Your Creative Heart* G. P. Putnam and Sons

Internet

Websites encouraging, exploring and developing creativity
www.creativityforlife.com
articles, tips, newsletter, motivation for creativity in life
www.creativityatwork.com
creativity and innovation in the workplace
www.creativitypool.com
a database of creative and original ideas
www.creativity-portal.com

Inspiration and support for artists, writers and others in the art mode
www.enchantedmind.com
to awaken your latent creativity
www.mycoted.com
creativity techniques
www.creativityworkshop.com
conducts classes on developing your creative forces
www.amcreativityassoc.org
non-profit association fostering the development of creative
    thinking

CHANGE

Bibliography/Recommended Reading

Library Information Professionals (1997) *Change As Opportunity: at the Crossroads* Special Libraries Association

Fullan, Michael (2001) *Leading in a Culture of Change* Jossey-Bass: 1st edition A book focusing on the dynamics of change from the leadership perspective

Price Waterhouse Coopers (2005) *Globalisation and Complexity.* A fascinating review of the 9th Annual Global CEO survey PWC undertakes. 1,400 CEOs spread across the globe are surveyed regarding global change in business. Heavy emphasis on the emerging markets in China, India, Russia and Brazil. Can be ordered free from Price Waterhouse Coopers at *www.pwc.com.* A must read.

Magazines online

The Futurist at *www.wfs.org/futurist.htm* The official organ of the World Futurist Society. The magazine forecasts trends and ideas

New Scientist at *www.newscientist.com* Offers best new ideas of the week

Gizmag at *http://www.gizmag.com/* Covers invention, innovation, and emerging technologies

ZZZ at *http://www.zzz.com.ru/* News, covers the latest in technology

Websites

http://www.forrester.com/my/1,,1-0,FF.html
http://www.jupiterresearch.com/bin/item.pl/home
http://www.gartner.com/

Organizations

National Bureau of Economic Research
   http://www.nber.org/
Marketing Research Association
   http://www.mra-net.org

SELF-ASSESSMENT

Bibliography/Recommended Reading

Jensen, Julie (2003) *I Don't Know What I Want, But I Know It's Not This,* Penguin Books. An excellent step by step guide to finding the work that's right for you

Lore, Nicholas (1998) *The Pathfinder: How to Choose or Change Your Career for a Lifetime of Satisfaction and Success* Fireside. Another excellent work on finding your way to that place that you were meant to occupy

Tieger, Paul D. and Barbara Barron-Tieger (2001) *Do What You Are: Discover the Perfect Career for You Through the Secrets of Personality Type*—Revised and Updated Edition. Featuring E-careers for the 21st Century. Little, Brown: 3rd edition Helps you find what you were meant to do by examining personality traits.

Internet

http://www.rileyguide.com/assess.html

http://www.fullcirc.com/community/assessmentlinks.htm

http://careerplanning.about.com/od/selfassessment/a/self_ assessment.htm

Thinking Positively

Books

Bibliography/Recommended Reading

Lewis, David and James Greene *Thinking Better* (1982) Rawson, Wade A good book on thinking better at any age

Murphy, Joseph (2001) *The Power of Your Subconscious Mind,* Revised, Bantam Books. A classic on the use of the subconscious. Fascinating insight on how the mind works and how we can use it to great advantage.

Hill, Napoleon (1960) *Think and Grow Rich* Fawcett. Another classic. At this time 43 printings on how to apply the mind, largely the subconscious, to achieve success in business.

Internet

http://www.thinking.net/

http://www.austhink.org/critical/

http://www.library.ucla.edu/libraries/college/help/critical/

http://www.uspto.gov/web/offices/ac/ahrpa/opa/projxl/ invthink/invthink.htm

http://www.studygs.net/genius.htm

http://www.virtualsalt.com/crebook2.htm

COMPUTER SUPPORT PROGRAMS

Speech recognition

Scansoft Dragon Naturally Speaking 8 at computer stores or online at *http://www.nuance.com/naturallyspeaking/* you can speak rather than type to create text. About $100.

Education

Video Professor at *www.videoprofessor.com*

Easy learning technique. Various subjects such as navigating the Internet, word processing programs, Web design, financial management.

FORMAT SUPPORT

Writing

Poynter, Dan (2003) *The Self-Publishing Manual,* Revised Para Publishing. The complete book on writing, printing and selling your own book. 430 pages. Available at www.parapublishing.com.

Cullins, Judy (2005) *Write Your eBook or other short book—fast* Skills Unlimited Publishing. A timely book on how to write and market a short book. Very helpful for Internet marketing. 116 pages. Available at *www.bookcoaching.com.* Inexpensive.

Johnson, Robert B. and Ron Pramschufer (2003) *Publishing Basics,* RJ Communications, LLC. A comprehensive guide for the neophyte. Very informative. 112 pages. Contact *www.booksjustbooks.com.* Will send for free.

Reiss, Fern (2003) *The Publishing Game, Publish a Book in Thirty Days.* Peanut Butter and Jelly Press. A day by day guide to self publishing your book. 256 pages. Available at *www.publishinggame.com.*

Ross, Tom and Marilyn Ross (2002) *The Complete Guide to Self Publishing* Fourth Ed. Writer's Digest Books. A very readable and complete book about everything you need to know about self-publishing.

Hupalo, Peter (2002) *How to Start & Run a Small Book Publishing Company* HCM publishing. This book is by someone who does it. Covers the day-to-day stuff other books do not. A must have if you are starting up.

Kampmann, Eric, *The Midpoint Handbook,* Beaufort Books.
Necessary reading for the self-publisher. Available at
Midpoint Trade Books, 27 West 20th St., New York, NY 10011

Kremer, John *1001 Ways to Market Your Books* Open Horizons,
Fifth Edition. The premier guide for marketing books. If you
are going to self-publish books be sure to get this.

WRITING SALES LETTERS

Books

Caples, John (1997) *Tested Advertising Methods* Prentice Hall.
One of the classics on writing ads and sales letters.

Collier, Robert (1937) *The Robert Collier Letter Book* Robert
Collier Publications. A compendium of the sales letters
Collier wrote that hold true to today's Internet needs.

Kennedy, Dan (2006) *The Ultimate Sales Letter, Attract New
Customers. Boost Your Sales* Adams Media 3rd Edition.
Good insight on writing sales letters in today's setting.

Course

Vitale, Joe *Hypnotic Writing* Known as Mr. Fire, Vitale has
put together an electronic course that is available at
http://www.mrfire.com/.

PUBLIC SPEAKING

Bibliography/Recommended Reading

Rogers, Natalie (2000) *The New Talk Power—The Mind Body Way To Speak Without Fear.* Capital Books(VA).

Carnegie, Dale (1985) *The Quick and Easy Way to Effective Speaking.* Revised to include modern techniques for dynamic communication. Pocket Books.

Walters, Lilly (1993) *Secrets of Successful Speakers* McGraw Hill. The art of motivating, captivating and persuading told by someone who does it for a living and has watched the heavyweights do it and shares with us how they do it.

Internet

How To Conquer Public Speaking Fear. An interesting report by Morton C. Orman, M.D. Helpful information worth knowing. Go to: *http://www.stresscure.com/jobstress/ speak.html*

Toastmaster International gives you tips on how to deal with fear if you are going to speak in public. Good advice from people who know how to deal with the subject. Go to *http://www.toastmasters.org/tips.asp*

AUDIO

Software For the Beginner

For the PC

Sony Sound Forge Audio Studio. A complete and easy-to-use application for Windows PCs. This single-track audio-recording and -editing program includes more than 30 built-in effects. Sony also offers, for a few dollars more, a live person telephone hand holder. Comes with a 1001 sound effects. You can have fun with this. About $70. At *www.sony.com*

For the Mac

BIAS Deck 3.5 LE turns your Mac into a full-fledged recording studio. Easily record up to 12 tracks, with full CD quality. It will edit your work instantly (while always being able to revert to your original recordings). About $70. At *www.bias.com*

Recommended Reading

Fisher, Jeffrey (2004) *Instant Sound Forge* CMP Books. This is a great book for Sound Forge users. Not only does it tell you what to do, it shows you how to hide mistakes and improve audio. A big help for the beginner.

VIDEO

Software

Pinnacle Studio Plus 9. Excellent for first time users. Easy to use. Broad feature set, particularly for audio and DVD authoring. Strong performance.

Magazines

Digital Video Editing at *http://www.digitalvideoediting.com/* If you are doing video on your website and you are editing yourself, this magazine will offer some interesting ideas.

PC Magazine at *http://www.pcmag.com.* This is very fine magazine for PC computer support. Keeps you abreast of the newest and the best of video and all other aspects as well.

Macworld at *http://www.macworld.com/* The Mac counterpart to *PC Magazine.* Like *PC Magazine,* an important source of information about the very thing that will be the cornerstone of your business.

Free Consultation

Members of The Twenty Per Cent Club can receive a free consultation for video editing by Emmy Award winning editor David Seeger and his staff. Go to *Careerofgold.com/twentypercentclub*

Seminars
Books

Gleeck, Fred (2001) *Marketing and Promoting your own Seminars and Workshops* Fast Forward Press.

Karasil, Paul (2004) *How to Make it Big in the Seminar Business* McGraw-Hill.

Tele-seminars
Providers

These companies will set you up for a conference.

Brainwave Communications. 2188 San Diego Ave., Suite P, San Diego, CA 92110 and at *www.bwc.com.*

e-teleconferencing a division of BudgetWare, Inc. 5531 Youngville Road, Springfield, TN 37172 at *http:// www.e-teleconferencing.com/*

WEBSITE DESIGN AND HOSTING

Self-Design

Homestead at *http://www.homestead.com/*

Homestead will host your site for about $240 a year. You design your own web page here with templates and ease.

Startlogic at *Startlogic.com*. Similar to Homestead with wide template selection and ease of design. Also about $240 a year with live telephone tech support.

Inexpensive Website Designers

www.heritagewebdesign.com

www.design.aplus.net

www.provenwebideas.com

www.cincystreetdesign.com

www.cybersharks.net

Inexpensive Website hosting

www.godaddy.com

www.hostmonster.com

www.startlogic.com

www.dot5hosting.com

www.hostmonster.com

www.midphase.com

BUSINESS ORGANIZATION

Business Plans and Organizational Procedures

Internet

U. S. Small Business Administration—Business Plan Basics. Shows you what you need to know when starting up and how to go about doing what you must do. Excellent site. For free business plans go to: *http://www.sba.gov/starting_ business/planning/basic.html*

U. S. Small Business Administration-Start up Information. Touches on all aspects from marketing to legal. Another free service from the U. S. Government. *http://www.sba.gov/ starting_business/index.html*

Entrepreneur Magazine is a very helpful source for the startup business, as well as the ongoing firm. A must for your list. *http://www.entrepreneur.com/*

The Wall Street Journal has a very good site for startup businesses, another must for your list. *http://www. startupjournal.com/*

IMPORTANT GOVERNMENT WEBSITES

FedWorld makes it easy to locate government information
http://www.fedworld.gov/

Official U. S. Executive Branch Websites

http://www.loc.gov/rr/news/fedgov.html
> The place to contact all the departments of government by Internet access.

http://www.gksoft.com/govt/en/us.html

Business.gov guides you through the maze of government rules and regulations and provides access to services and resources to help you start, grow, and succeed in business.
http://www.business.gov/

Science.gov is a gateway to authoritative selected science information provided by U. S. government agencies including research and development results.
http://www.science.gov/

The gateway to statistics from over 100 U. S. federal agencies.
http://www.fedstats.gov

U. S. Government Science and
Technology Gateway and Portal Websites

Sites that pull together information from across government
   agencies.
   http://www.scitechresources.gov/

Portals to the World contains selective links providing authoritative, in-depth information about the nations and other
   areas of the world.
   http://www.loc.gov/rr/international/po

INDEX

You Need Not Be Alone

Starting up a new business can be a lonely business. But if you are planning to start a career of gold you can have company. To help you along and to connect you with people who will be doing what you do, go to *www.careerofgold.com* and then go to the 20 Per Cent Club. There you can get questions answered, guidance given and the company of others.

So don't delay. Check in and get going on the new career that may bring an exciting change to your life.

Quick Order Form

Today's Books. An imprint of History Publishing Company, LLC

Fax orders: 845-359-8282. Fax this completed form.

Telephone: Call toll free 888-359-8555. Have credit card handy.

E-mail orders: orders@careerofgold.com

Postal Orders: Today's Books, P. O. Box 700, Palisades, NY 10964

Please send me:

_____copies of *Career of Gold*

Payment: ☐ Check   ☐ Credit card

☐ Visa   ☐ MasterCard   ☐ American Express

Name on card _____

Number on card _____

Expiration Date _____

Shipment by USPS

Please inquire about our volume discount
for purchases of *Career of Gold*.

*Small opportunities are often the
beginning of great enterprises.*
—Demosthenes

*Opportunity is missed by most people because it is
dressed in overalls and looks like work.*
—Thomas Edison

*There is no security on this earth,
there is only opportunity.*
—General Douglas Mc Arthur

ABOUT THE AUTHOR

Don Bracken launched his first career of gold at age 55 as a marketing and sales expert helping others find success. He built, developed and organized a company servicing the major Northeastern market in such commodities as telecommunications and health insurance, and in the process guided hundreds of men and women toward their financial goals. At age 65 he formed another company, History Publishing Company, a firm catering to the development of classroom aids through the use of modern technology.

Don Bracken has several years experience in the corporate world as well, and has written articles on marketing, economics and education for major newspapers and trade magazines.

He is a graduate of Manhattan College where he studied economics and marketing and was inducted into *Alpha Delta Sigma,* the prestigious marketing fraternity.

NOTES

NOTES

NOTES

NOTES